MASTER
BUIL

Other Works by Wallace Shawn

SCREENPLAYS:
My Dinner with André
by Wallace Shawn and André Gregory
Marie and Bruce
by Wallace Shawn and Tom Cairns
A Master Builder

TRANSLATIONS:
The Mandrake by Niccolò Machiavelli
The Threepenny Opera by Bertolt Brecht

OPERA LIBRETTI:
In the Dark, music by Allen Shawn
The Music Teacher, music by Allen Shawn

ESSAYS:
Essays

PLAYS:
The Hotel Play
Our Late Night
A Thought in Three Parts
Marie and Bruce
Aunt Dan and Lemon
The Fever
The Designated Mourner
Grasses of a Thousand Colors

A MASTER BUILDER

By Henrik Ibsen

*Translated and Adapted
by Wallace Shawn*

THEATRE COMMUNICATIONS GROUP
NEW YORK
2014

A Master Builder is published by Theatre Communications Group, Inc., 520 Eighth Avenue, 24th Floor, New York, NY 10018-4156

The publication of *A Master Builder*, by Wallace Shawn, through TCG's Book Program, is made possible in part by the New York State Council on the Arts with the support of Governor Andrew Cuomo and the New York State Legislature.

Special thanks to Jujamcyn Theaters for their generous support of this publication.

TCG books are exclusively distributed to the book trade by Consortium Book Sales and Distribution.

LIBRARY OF CONGRESS CATALOGING-IN-PUBLICATION DATA
Ibsen, Henrik, 1828–1906.
[Bygmester Solness. English.]
A Master Builder / by Henrik Ibsen ; translated and adapted by
Wallace Shawn.
pages cm
ISBN 978-1-55936-449-2 (paperback)
ISBN 978-1-55936-756-1 (ebook)
I. Shawn, Wallace. II. Title.
PT8859.A31   2013
839.822'6—dc23   2013039473

Text design and composition by Lisa Govan
Cover design by Mark Melnick
Front cover: Lisa Joyce, Wallace Shawn and Julie Hagerty in *A Master Builder*,
a film by Jonathan Demme, created for the stage by André Gregory;
cinematography by Declan Quinn / Courtesy of the Ibsen Project LLC
© 2014. Back cover: photographs by YouWorkForThem.

First Edition, June 2014

To André Gregory,
companion of pleasure
in the magic garden of theater

and

To Allen Shawn,
noble and tireless comrade
on the road of life

Contents

A
MASTER
BUILDER

Production History

André Gregory's production of *A Master Builder* was not done in a theater (at least, as of 2014 it has not been done), but instead it was made into a film with the following cast:

Nurse Olga: Sheilagh Weymouth
Nurse Nora: Joanna Howard
Nurse Myrtle: Winsome Brown
Nurse Ingrid: Marjorie Graham
Nurse Number Five/Hilde Wangel: Lisa Joyce
Halvard Solness: Wallace Shawn
Aline Solness: Julie Hagerty
Knut Brovik: André Gregory
Ragnar Brovik: Jeff Biehl
Kaya Fosli: Emily Cass McDonnell
Dr. Herdal: Larry Pine

Created and directed for the stage by: André Gregory
Assistant to the director: David Skeist
Norwegian expertise and wisdom: Sandra Saari
Profound thanks: George Gaynes, David Shapiro, Leslie Silva, Brooke Smith
Music for the nurses: Bruce Odland
Supplementary acting: Leigh Wade

The film was presented by The Ibsen Project/Clinica Estetico
in association with Westward Productions and Scott Griffin
Costumes: Dona Granata
Music: Zafer Tawil, Thom O'Connor, Suzana Perić
Production Design: Eugene Lee
Editor: Tim Squyres, A.C.E.
Director of Photography: Declan Quinn, A.S.C.
Co-Executive Producers: Caroline Baron, Anthony Weintraub,
    Annette Solakoglu, Kemal Solakoglu
Executive Producers: Ron Bozman, Beau Willimon,
    Jordan Tappis, Declan Quinn, Scott Griffin
Associate Producer: Jacob Burns Film Center
Produced by Rocco Caruso, André Gregory, Wallace Shawn
Screenplay: Wallace Shawn
Director: Jonathan Demme

Cast of Characters

NURSE OLGA

NURSE NORA

NURSE MYRTLE

NURSE INGRID

NURSE NUMBER FIVE (later HILDE WANGEL)

HALVARD SOLNESS

ALINE SOLNESS

KNUT BROVIK

RAGNAR BROVIK

KAYA FOSLI

DR. HERDAL

Note

Nurse Olga, Nurse Nora, Nurse Myrtle and Nurse Ingrid later become women of the town. They may also possibly serve as stage managers and stage hands, they may operate the lights, etc.

PART ONE

Some chairs, a small table and a tall, mechanical hospital-style bed, with a footstool at the side. In the bed is a man of late middle age. He is attached by tubes and wires to an IV and a monitor. He wears a bathrobe. There are five nurses in uniforms who are taking care of the man in the bed, and for a while we watch a quiet, dimly lit tableau in which they slowly take notes on the readings of the monitor, carry in different medicine bottles and remove others, etc.

NURSE OLGA *(To the other nurses)*: Well, I'm never wrong about these things, and I say he has hardly any time left at all.

NURSE NORA: Really?

NURSE MYRTLE: He seems so healthy . . .

NURSE OLGA: No, no. The signs are there. Look.

NURSE NORA: Oh.

NURSE MYRTLE: I see.

NURSE INGRID: I hadn't realized . . .

NURSE NUMBER FIVE: Does he know?

NURSE OLGA: Well, no one's said anything to him, but deep down I think he does know. Here— *(She gives a glass to Nurse Number Five)* —give him this if he wakes up.

(Nurse Olga exits, followed by Nurse Nora, Nurse Myrtle and Nurse Ingrid. The patient wakes up, and Nurse Number Five hands him the glass.)

NURSE NUMBER FIVE: Here.

(The patient takes the glass, drinks, looks at Nurse Number Five, then falls back to sleep. A middle-aged woman comes in and sits in a chair by the bed. Then an elderly man, a young man and a young woman come in and sit in chairs on a different side of the bed. Nurse Number Five does a couple of things around the bed and goes out. The actor who plays Dr. Herdal comes in and speaks to the audience.)

ACTOR: Good evening, friends. Thank you for coming to see us. Now, in order to prevent hours of confusion, I'm going to tell you who all these people are, before we begin the play, and I'll start by telling you that the person in the bed is called Halvard Solness. Halvard Solness is what is called a "master builder," which is sort of midway between being an architect and being what we would call a builder or contractor. And this is his wife, Aline. *(Indicating her)* Halvard and Aline Solness live in a large house in a rather small town, and Halvard Solness has been for many years by far the most successful builder in the town. He keeps his office in a wing of his house, but since he's been ill he's been running his business out of his bedroom. Now, these three people all work for Halvard Solness. *(Indicating them)* This older man is called Knut Brovik. At one time, Knut Brovik was the town's most successful builder, and at that time Halvard Solness worked for him, but now he works for Halvard Solness. Also working in Halvard

Solness's office are Ragnar Brovik, Knut's son, and Ragnar's fiancée, Kaya Fosli. I play Doctor Herdal, and I'm
Aline Solness's best friend as well as Solness's doctor. As the
play begins, Old Brovik, Ragnar and Kaya are waiting for
Halvard Solness to wake up, because Old Brovik, who's not
in good health, very much wants to discuss something with
him. It's evening, and Brovik is feeling particularly unwell.

*(The actor playing Dr. Herdal leaves, along with Aline
Solness. Brovik, Ragnar and Kaya speak rather quietly, as
people do at the bedside of someone who's ill or asleep.)*

BROVIK: I don't know how much longer—I'll be able to—stand
this! —My chest—
KAYA: Oh God, it's really bad tonight . . .
BROVIK: It's—I think it's—getting worse—every day!
RAGNAR: Why don't you just go home, Father? Go to bed and
try to sleep a little . . .
BROVIK *(Impatiently)*: Oh, you mean just "lie down for a little
rest"? When I lie down, then the other thing starts, the—
the choking—I—
KAYA: Maybe you could just take a little walk or something . . .
RAGNAR: That's a good idea, Father. I'd come with you . . .
BROVIK *(Heavily)*: No! I have to speak to our great—
employer!—there are things I'm going to say to him—
very frankly—
KAYA: But—shouldn't you maybe wait for a while?—
RAGNAR: It might be better to wait a bit, Father, because—
BROVIK *(Laughing, but breathing with difficulty)*: I may not
have all that much—time—in which—to wait! Heh! Heh!

(Halvard Solness wakes up.)

SOLNESS: So!—er—has anyone been here—looking for me?
RAGNAR: Oh—yes—er—that young couple came by, you know,
the people who want to build that villa out at Lovstrand.

SOLNESS: Oh—them. Well, they're going to have to wait. I'm not sure about the design . . . I—

RAGNAR: Well, they kept saying that it was terribly important for them to get the drawings soon . . .

SOLNESS: Is that right? . . .

BROVIK: Well, they said they were just so eager to move into their own place, they—

SOLNESS: Yes, they're so goddamned eager to move into it that they really don't care what kind of place it is! A place, a *place*, a place to move into. That's not the same as a *home*—don't they see that? Well, that's absolutely fine, but then they should go to somebody else. Leave me out of it. Why don't you just tell them *that* when they come back next time?

BROVIK: Go to somebody else? You mean—you'd give up the job? . . .

SOLNESS: For God's sake yes! Yes! Yes! I mean, if they want me to put up a building without taking the time to work out a meaningful design—I mean, I don't even really *know* these people!

BROVIK: Oh, they're very good people—Ragnar knows them— he's visited them often. They're very trustworthy, reliable people . . .

SOLNESS: Oh—reliable! Reliable! I'm sure they're *reliable*— I'm sure they'll *pay* me—that's not what I'm talking about! My God—don't *you* understand me either? . . . I don't want to deal with strangers anymore! Let them go to anyone they like—I really don't care.

BROVIK: Do you honestly mean that?

SOLNESS: Yes, I do. For God's sake . . .

(No one speaks for a while.)

BROVIK: Mmm—by the way, I was wondering if I could have a few moments to discuss something with you?

SOLNESS: Of course—please.

BROVIK *(To Kaya)*: Will you give us a minute, dear?

KAYA: I—I don't—

BROVIK: Please. Just let us talk together here for a moment, will you? Please.

(Ragnar walks out briskly. Kaya gestures helplessly and leaves.)

I don't want the poor children to know how sick I am.

SOLNESS: Yes. You've been looking awfully weak, recently . . .

BROVIK: I'm not going to be around much longer. That's the reality. Each day I seem to lose something or other—one more faculty—it's all going—all my strength—I—

SOLNESS: Mmm-hmm. Yes?

BROVIK: And you see, what weighs on me so terribly is— What's going to become of Ragnar?

SOLNESS: Well, I mean—he can stay here with me for as long as he likes . . .

BROVIK: But you see, apparently he feels that he just *can't* stay any longer . . .

SOLNESS: What are you saying? Does he want a raise?

BROVIK: No, it's more that the day has to come when he will have the opportunity to do his own work . . .

SOLNESS: I see. And are you positive that he has all the particular qualities he would need for that?

BROVIK *(After a pause)*: No, that's what's so awful—I'm *not* positive. Even I myself have begun to have doubts about his abilities, because *you* have never said one single encouraging word about him! And yet I know in my heart that he *is talented.*

SOLNESS: Well, but he just hasn't fully mastered that much of the discipline—I mean, he knows how to draw, but—

BROVIK: You hadn't mastered that much of the discipline either when you were working for me, but that didn't stop you from plunging in and—and seizing the moment *(Breathing heavily)* —and making a tremendous impression on everyone. —It certainly didn't stop you from luring away the wind that was in *my* sails at the time—it didn't stop you from racing past everyone around you—

SOLNESS: Yes, it worked out that way, didn't it?

BROVIK: Yes it did. That's the way it worked out . . . But seriously, you *can't* have the heart to let me go to my grave without having the chance to see what Ragnar can make of himself. He needs to get married—he—

SOLNESS: Is that what Kaya wants?

BROVIK: Well, maybe she's a little less passionate about it than he is, but Ragnar talks about it all day long! He needs to be married, and *I* need to see some work that my boy has done!

SOLNESS: Yes, but goddammit, I can't bring commissions down out of the sky for him!

BROVIK: He could obtain an excellent commission right now, as a matter of fact—an important project—something really worthwhile.

SOLNESS: He could?

BROVIK: Yes, if you would give your approval.

SOLNESS: And what project is that?

BROVIK: He could build that villa out at Lovstrand!

SOLNESS: What? But I'm going to be doing that project myself!

BROVIK: But—but you—you no longer have any desire to do it.

SOLNESS: No longer have any desire to do it? Who in the world had the *audacity* to tell you that?

BROVIK: You said it yourself two minutes ago.

SOLNESS: Oh, for God's sake, I was joking! . . . But seriously, could Ragnar really get that commission?

BROVIK: Oh yes—he knows the family well. And, actually, you know, for his own amusement, he actually did do some sketches of some things he *might* do, you know, some drawings, and a few estimates of—

SOLNESS: And you think that the family was pleased by these—drawings?

BROVIK: Oh yes. I mean, if you would just look them over and approve them—

SOLNESS: Then they'd actually let Ragnar complete the building?

BROVIK: Well, they liked what he proposed to them very much. They said they thought it was original, something really new . . .

SOLNESS: Oh! I see! Really new! Not like the sort of very conventional buildings *I* always build, with their flavor of the past, their sort of—

BROVIK: Look, you're—

SOLNESS: So, it was actually Ragnar they came here to see.

BROVIK: No, no. They came to see you. Really. I mean, they simply wanted to ask if you might be willing to step aside and—

SOLNESS: Step aside!

BROVIK: In case you found that Ragnar's drawings—

SOLNESS: Step aside! Step aside? For Ragnar?

BROVIK: They simply meant—you know, to remove your name from the agreement, so that Ragnar—

SOLNESS: I understand what they meant! . . . Well well—so the moment has come when Master Builder Halvard Solness starts to "step aside" to make way for those who are younger. That's wonderful!

BROVIK: But my God, surely there's room for more than one single solitary—

SOLNESS: No—not really. No, there isn't as much room as you think. No. But in any case, it's irrelevant, because I'm not going to step aside.

BROVIK: So am I really going to leave this life without the happiness that comes from—without the sense of confidence—I mean, am I going to die without having been able to see a single piece of work that's been done by my son? So that I can truly believe in his talent and his future? Is that the way it's going to be? . . . Answer me! Am I actually going to leave the world like that?—with such a terrible sense of deprivation?

SOLNESS: You're going to leave the world—with as much dignity as you can find in yourself.

BROVIK: Well— All right, then. *(He starts to leave)*

SOLNESS: Because I can't do anything else!—don't you see that? I can only be what I am! And I can't change what I am— I can't. I can't.

BROVIK: No, no—of course. You can't, of course.

(A silence. Solness calls to Ragnar.)

SOLNESS: Ragnar!

(Ragnar, Kaya, Nurse Olga and Nurse Nora come in. The nurses examine Solness.)

RAGNAR *(To Brovik)*: What is it, Father?

BROVIK: We're going to go now.

NURSE NORA *(To Solness)*: Please don't get too excited. It's not good for you.

(The two nurses go out.)

RAGNAR: Come along, Kaya.

SOLNESS: No, Miss Fosli can't leave yet. I have a letter that has to be written, I'm afraid.

BROVIK *(To Solness)*: So. Good night. Sleep well—if you can.

SOLNESS: Yes, good night.

(Brovik and Ragnar go out.)

KAYA *(Uncertainly)*: So—is there a letter?—

SOLNESS *(Shouts)*: No of course there isn't! . . . Kaya!

KAYA: Yes?

SOLNESS: Come over here!

KAYA: Yes?—

SOLNESS: Come *over* here.

KAYA *(She comes closer)*: Tell me—what you want . . .

SOLNESS *(Looks at her for a while)*: Are you the one I should thank for this—situation?

KAYA: No!— Please—you mustn't—

SOLNESS: I mean, you're terribly eager to be married, it seems.

KAYA *(Softly)*: Well, Ragnar and I have been engaged for four or five years . . .

SOLNESS: Yes?

KAYA: Well, he and his father keep talking about it, and eventually I suppose I'll have to give in.

SOLNESS: And of course you have a certain *affection* for Ragnar . . .

KAYA: I used to have a great *deal* of affection for him, before I came to work for you.

SOLNESS: But you don't anymore?

KAYA *(Passionately)*: I—I only care about one person—one—I don't care about anybody else. And I never will.

SOLNESS: Well, you say that. But then at the same time you seem to be making plans to leave me, aren't you?

KAYA: But—but couldn't I still work here even if—?

SOLNESS: No! No! It can't happen that way! If Ragnar goes off and sets up on his own, then he's going to need you himself, don't you see that?

KAYA: But I don't think I can be separated from you! I just—it's impossible!

SOLNESS: Look, go ahead and get married if that's what you want, but— *(Changes his tone)* I mean—can't you just convince him to stay here? He has a good position here. And that's the only way I'll be able to keep you with me, Kaya—my dear little Kaya—

KAYA: Oh, it would be so wonderful if it could turn out like that . . .

(He touches her.)

SOLNESS: Because I can't—not have you. Do you understand? I have to have you with me. Every day. You have to be with me . . .

KAYA: Oh God—God—

SOLNESS (*Kissing her*): Kaya—Kaya—

KAYA: How kind you are—so incredibly kind—

SOLNESS (*Suddenly*): Get up! Get up!

VOICE OF MRS. SOLNESS (*From a distance*): Halvard?

SOLNESS: Yes, dear?

(*Mrs. Solness comes in.*)

MRS. SOLNESS: Ah—I guess I've come at an—inconvenient moment . . .

SOLNESS: No, not at all. Miss Fosli just has a short letter to write, and—

MRS. SOLNESS: Oh, yes—

(*Silence.*)

SOLNESS: Did you need me for something, Aline?

MRS. SOLNESS: No, I just wanted to say that Doctor Herdal is here— He came over to see me, and he just wanted to say hello to you at the same time.

SOLNESS: Oh good, good.

(*Mrs. Solness goes out.*)

KAYA: My God, I feel as if your wife is just—thinking terrible thoughts about me.

SOLNESS: Oh no, no. I'm sure she's just thinking the same things she always thinks. But anyway—it's probably time for you to head on home . . .

KAYA: Yes—yes—

SOLNESS: And I want you to settle that whole thing with Ragnar. Did you hear what I said?

KAYA: Oh, I wish it were in my power to *do* that—I—

SOLNESS: I'm saying that I have to have it settled! Please give me an answer—by tomorrow!

KAYA (*Full of anxiety*): Well, if it can't be done any other way,

I'll happily just—end the whole thing with him—I'd—

SOLNESS: End the whole thing? Are you completely out of your mind? *End the whole thing?*

KAYA: Yes, I would, because—I have to stay here—I can't leave!—I—

SOLNESS: But for Christ's sake, I don't want Ragnar to—

KAYA: What? What? You—?

SOLNESS: Kaya! Please! Try to understand! I'm trying to tell you—I have to have you. —More than anything, Kaya. Please, dear.

KAYA: Yes. Yes. *(Pause)* Well—good night.

SOLNESS: Good night, dear Kaya. *(As she's about to go)* No—wait a minute! Wait. Please—bring me Ragnar's drawings.

KAYA *(Happy)*: Oh—yes. That's wonderful. Really. *(She brings him a large portfolio of drawings)*

SOLNESS: I mean, for your sake, Kaya—I can at least—

KAYA: Yes . . . Well—good night then . . . Think kind thoughts about me.

SOLNESS: Always—my sweet little Kaya—always—

(Mrs. Solness and Dr. Herdal come in.)

MRS. SOLNESS: I can't keep the doctor any longer, Halvard—

SOLNESS: Yes, by all means come in!

MRS. SOLNESS *(To Kaya)*: All finished with that letter, Miss Fosli?

KAYA *(Confused)*: That—letter?—er—

SOLNESS: Oh it was just a short note, really, you know—

MRS. SOLNESS: Oh yes—a short note—ha ha ha—yes yes—one of those really short ones—

SOLNESS: Well, you may as well go now, I suppose, Miss Fosli. And—er—be sure you're on time tomorrow morning!— heh heh—

KAYA: Oh yes, I certainly will be! Good night, Mrs. Solness. *(She goes out)*

MRS. SOLNESS: That must really be a good thing for you, Halvard, to have found that young woman.

SOLNESS: Oh yes, yes, she's just so useful in so many ways.

MRS. SOLNESS: Yes, she seems as if she would be.

DR. HERDAL: And she's—er—good at bookkeeping?

SOLNESS: Well she's had an awful lot of practice at bookkeeping, of course, in these last two years. But the other thing
is, you see, she's such a kind person—she's—ready to do
whatever comes up that needs to be done . . .

MRS. SOLNESS: Yes, that must certainly give you a feeling of
comfort . . .

SOLNESS: Mm—it does. It's been a long time since anyone's
been available to look after my needs, you know . . .

MRS. SOLNESS: Well, but how can you say that, Halvard?

SOLNESS: Oh now, Aline—ha ha ha—well, please forgive
me—ha ha ha—

MRS. SOLNESS: So! —Doctor—will you be returning later to
have some supper?

DR. HERDAL: As soon as I've completed my house calls, I'll
come right back.

MRS. SOLNESS: Good. Good.

*(She goes out. The doctor is about to follow when Solness
stops him.)*

SOLNESS: Pardon me—could I possibly have a few words with
you?

DR. HERDAL: Of course—that would be delightful.

SOLNESS: So. Please sit down . . .

(The doctor sits by the bed.)

So—er—now tell me . . . Did you notice anything in
particular just now—about Aline? I mean, in relation to
me . . .

DR. HERDAL: Well *yes*, for God's sake—I mean, one could
hardly help noticing that she—

SOLNESS: Yes?

DR. HERDAL: Well, your wife doesn't seem to be terribly fond of
that Miss Fosli of yours—aha ha ha—

SOLNESS: Well—

DR. HERDAL: I mean, it's not that surprising that she doesn't
particularly like the fact—that you spend every single day
in the company—of another woman—

SOLNESS: Well, but that happens to be something that can't be
changed.

DR. HERDAL: Why not? Couldn't you find a male secretary?
I mean, if your wife really feels—in other words, she's a
very fragile woman, and if it's something, you know, that
she really can't bear, I mean, to look at this young girl—

SOLNESS: Oh for God's sake—so what? Who cares? Do you
think I care about that? Well, I do, in a way. I do, obviously.
But the situation is what it is.

DR. HERDAL: You mean—there's no alternative?

SOLNESS: That's right. There's no alternative.

DR. HERDAL: Hm. Well of course, women's perceptions are
often—mm—infuriatingly accurate on certain topics—

SOLNESS: Yes?

DR. HERDAL: And so when your wife happens to find that she
just can't stand that Kaya Fosli—er—well, don't you think
that maybe there's some sort of a *basis*—for—that sort
of—involuntary reflex of—antipathy?

SOLNESS: No, no. Not at all.

DR. HERDAL: I see. So there's just no basis for your wife's feeling
at all, in other words.

SOLNESS: Only her own suspiciousness, I suppose.

(Silence.)

DR. HERDAL: Of course I know that you've come in contact with
a great many women in the course of your life.

SOLNESS: Yes.

DR. HERDAL: And you've been rather fond of some of them.

SOLNESS: Mmmm.

DR. HERDAL: So I mean, in this case—

SOLNESS: I said, no. But seriously, there *is* something that I very much want to discuss with you. I would like to tell you—a very strange story—I mean, if you'd be willing to listen to it . . .

DR. HERDAL: I'm always happy to listen to a strange story.

SOLNESS: Very well then. *(Pause)* I'm sure you remember that many years ago I brought both Knut Brovik and his son over to work for me at a time when everything had gone terribly wrong for the old man.

DR. HERDAL: Yes . . .

SOLNESS: Well, at a certain point, a few years after that, Ragnar suddenly came up with the idea of getting married and leaving my office to set up an office of his own. But I needed Ragnar to stay with me, because he happens to be extremely clever about calculating, you know, the volume of things and the carrying capacity of this and that and all that sort of tedious detail.

DR. HERDAL: Well, that's an important element of your business—yes—

SOLNESS: But you see, listen to what I'm trying to tell you. One day, a young woman whom I'd never seen before came to visit Ragnar here, over there in the office, and this turned out to be Kaya Fosli, Ragnar's fiancée. Well, when I saw how incredibly infatuated with each other she and Ragnar were, the idea came to me: if I could get this girl to come work here in the office, then maybe Ragnar would stay here, too.

DR. HERDAL: Yes, I see . . .

SOLNESS: So I stood there staring at her, wishing I could think of how to persuade her to work here. And then we were introduced, but we had no conversation of any kind. And then she went away . . . Well, the next evening, after Brovik and Ragnar had gone home—she came here again, and—and—just as if I'd already made an arrangement with her, she asked me what her new responsibilities would be,

and whether she could start work immediately the next
morning. But I had never asked her to work here!

DR. HERDAL: My goodness . . .

SOLNESS: And then, almost as soon as she started working
for me, she seemed to sort of drift away from Ragnar—
and—

DR. HERDAL: —and she drifted over towards—you, perhaps?

SOLNESS: I mean, I know she can actually *feel* it if I look at her
from behind. And whenever I come *near* her—she starts
to shake—she literally *trembles* . . . I mean, seriously, how
can you *account* for that?

DR. HERDAL: Oh, well—I'm sure there's a scientific explanation for it out there somewhere—aha ha ha ha!—ha ha
ha ha—

SOLNESS: No, I *mean*, what made her imagine I had *said* these
things to her which in fact I had only *thought?*—things I'd
said *silently*—inside my head—to *myself?* I mean, what
can you say about that? Can you possibly explain something like that, Doctor Herdal?

DR. HERDAL: Hm—I wouldn't want even to *speculate* about
that . . .

SOLNESS: Of course. That's just what I would have expected
you to say. It can't be explained. *And* it's left me in such
a horrible situation. Every day, I come in, and I have to
pretend that I—I—I just—it's a terrible thing to do to
this sweet little creature, but I can't *stop* doing it, because
if she were ever to leave me, then Ragnar would go, too!

DR. HERDAL: So you've allowed your wife to believe that you
really—

SOLNESS: Yes!

DR. HERDAL: But why?

SOLNESS: Well, there's a sort of wonderful well-deserved punishment that I can inflict on myself by allowing Aline to
condemn me when she really shouldn't . . .

DR. HERDAL: You know, I have to admit—I don't understand
what you're saying.

SOLNESS: You don't? But it's like paying a sort of tiny install-
ment on an enormous debt . . . and the tiny payment—well,
it eases one's mind a little. One can catch one's breath—
breathe more freely for a moment. You understand.

DR. HERDAL: Mm—not really, to be honest.

SOLNESS: Well—all right. All right. So shall we be absolutely
frank with each other for a moment? What do you think?
You see, I would like you, honestly, to tell me—just tell me
very directly—about some of the—some of the concerns
you've had recently—about me . . .

DR. HERDAL: What do you mean?

SOLNESS: You see, I've already seen it, I've seen it very clearly—

DR. HERDAL: Seen what?

SOLNESS: Well, I've seen you—watching me . . .

DR. HERDAL: What do you mean, watching you?

SOLNESS: Oh for Christ's sake—tell me! Haven't you begun to
think the very same thing that Aline thinks?

DR. HERDAL: Well—what would that be?

SOLNESS: She's started to think that in some way—or to some
degree—I'm—mentally sick . . .

DR. HERDAL: Mentally sick? What? She has absolutely never
said a *word* to me about anything like that. And it's never
occurred to me either. I've never thought for a second that
anything's wrong with you mentally.

SOLNESS: Is that right? Well, I think you're just reluctant to admit
what you think, because for all these years you've always
seen me as "Halvard Solness," this terribly fortunate man,
for whom everything has worked out well, and after all,
how could such a terribly fortunate man be mentally sick?

DR. HERDAL: Well, would that be some sort of an illusion, then?
Aren't you a terribly fortunate man? It seems to me that
you've experienced good fortune to an almost unbelievable extent, frankly.

*(Some strange music—like a sort of weird, unearthly vil-
lage band—starts playing rather loudly.)*

SOLNESS: Yes—I know that. Damn—what's that music?
DR. HERDAL: What music?
SOLNESS: Who's playing that?
DR. HERDAL: I don't hear anything.

(Solness seems to fall unconscious.)

Solness?

(Dr. Herdal touches Solness.)

What's going on?

(Dr. Herdal calls out for one of the nurses.)

Ingrid?

(Nurse Ingrid comes in.)

There's a blue bottle with a red label in my bag—I think it's in the spare room next to the dining room. Please hurry.

(She hurries out.)

Solness?

(The music stops. Solness wakes up.)

Are you all right?

(Solness doesn't know what's happened.)

SOLNESS: Am I all right? Of course. I'm fine.
DR. HERDAL: But—you were out cold for a moment there. Just all of a sudden—

SOLNESS: What are you talking about? I was listening to you telling me what a fortunate man I am.

DR. HERDAL: Well—

SOLNESS: No, but really, tell me—please go on—tell me what makes you feel that I'm such a fortunate man.

DR. HERDAL: Well—obviously—you've had a lot of good luck in your life. I mean—well—first, when that ugly old *mansion* burned down—ha ha ha—that place looked like a thieves' castle in a fairy tale—ha ha ha—

SOLNESS: Please! That was Aline's family home! It—

DR. HERDAL: Well, yes, for Aline it must have been a very sorrowful event—very painful, I'm sure . . .

SOLNESS: Well, she still hasn't recovered from it after all these years—ten or eleven years . . .

DR. HERDAL: And what happened afterwards was terrible . . .

SOLNESS: Yes . . .

DR. HERDAL: But that fire, really, was good luck for you! I mean, that fire actually made everything possible, didn't it, really? You were just a poor boy from the country!—ha ha ha—and now you are absolutely the leading man in your field! You are!

SOLNESS: Yes. And that's exactly what's kept me in such an awful state of uninterrupted anxiety . . .

DR. HERDAL: Anxiety? Because you've had good luck?

SOLNESS: Yes—don't you see it?—I'm in a state of unbearable agitation that starts the minute I wake up every morning, and it doesn't stop until I fall asleep at night. Because I know that my luck is going to turn around, it's going to spin itself out in the opposite direction.

(As Solness and Dr. Herdal talk, the nurses come in, move furniture around, and then leave.)

DR. HERDAL: But—why do you think that? What would make that happen?

SOLNESS: Well, that whole group of younger people will begin the process, I know that.

DR. HERDAL: I have to say, I think that's absurd. Your position in this community is absolutely unshakable—it's—

SOLNESS: No, it isn't. I feel that moment, coming towards me, when everything's going to change. One or another of those young people is going to just ask me to—"step aside"—and a whole process will start, and that will be that. You know what they say: "The younger generation will just show up one day and knock on the door . . ."

DR. HERDAL: Ha ha ha— Well, what if they do? Aha ha ha—

SOLNESS: Well, that will simply be the end of "Master Builder Solness," that's all I'm saying. You know, that will simply be the end of "Master Builder Solness," that's all I'm saying.

(Strange music fades in again.)

That will simply be the end of— *(He stops speaking)*

DR. HERDAL: Solness? Solness? *(He calls out)* Ingrid? I need that blue bottle! *(He touches Solness)* Solness?

(Solness seems to wake up. The nurses come in and examine him. We are now in Solness's dream, which continues until the last moments of the play.)

SOLNESS: "The younger generation will just show up one day and knock on the door . . ."

DR. HERDAL: Well, what if they do?

SOLNESS: Well, that will simply be the end of "Master Builder Solness," that's all I'm saying.

(The sound of knocking.)

Huh?

DR. HERDAL: What?

(The nurses leave.)

SOLNESS: Come in!

(Hilde Wangel—previously Nurse Number Five—comes in. She is around twenty-two. She is now dressed informally, in a revealing outfit. She looks like she's been walking for a while. She carries a few possessions, economically packed. The lights change completely and are now much brighter. The music slowly starts to fade out. Solness gets out of bed and stands up, easily pulling off his tubes and wires. He leaves his bathrobe behind and is fully dressed.)

HILDE: Hello.

SOLNESS: Hello . . .

HILDE *(Laughs)*: I almost thought you didn't recognize me.

SOLNESS: Ha ha ha— No, no . . . Although I have to admit—

DR. HERDAL: Well, *I* certainly recognize you!

(The music is gone.)

HILDE *(Delighted)*: Oh! It's you!

DR. HERDAL: Yes! It's me! Aha ha ha— *(To Solness)* Yes, we met this summer up at one of those hostels in the mountains! *(To Hilde)* I've always wanted to know where that whole group of ladies went—what *happened* to them?—aha ha ha—

HILDE: Oh, they all left the hotel, for some unknown reason—

DR. HERDAL: They probably weren't crazy about listening to us having so much fun in the evenings! Aha ha ha ha—

HILDE: No they certainly weren't! Ha ha ha—

DR. HERDAL *(Wags his finger at her)*: You . . . Now you have to admit that you were toying with all of us, weren't you?— that's right—you were playing games with all of us—

HILDE: Oh well, it was certainly a lot more fun than sitting with those ladies and knitting winter stockings!

DR. HERDAL: I understand! I understand!

(Silence.)

SOLNESS: Mm—so—er—let me guess—have you possibly just arrived in our town—this evening?

HILDE: I've just arrived this *moment*, as a matter of fact.

DR. HERDAL: And did you come entirely *alone*, Miss Wangel?

HILDE: Oh yes. I certainly did.

SOLNESS: Wangel? Your name is Wangel?

HILDE: Well I believe it is, if I'm not wrong.

SOLNESS: But—could you possibly be the daughter of the District Doctor up at Lysanger?

HILDE: Why—who else's daughter could I be?

SOLNESS: Well, then we *met* each other up there—the summer when I was staying there, and I built the tower for the old church . . .

HILDE: Yes. That was when we met.

SOLNESS: Well, that was a long time ago.

HILDE: It was *ten years* ago.

SOLNESS: Yes—ten years ago you would have been just a child, I imagine . . .

HILDE: Well, I was—twelve years old . . .

(Pause.)

DR. HERDAL: So, is this the first time you've ever been to our town, Miss Wangel?

HILDE: Yes, it certainly is.

SOLNESS: Then perhaps—er—you don't know anybody here . . .

HILDE: No one but you. *(Pause)* You—and your wife.

SOLNESS: Oh—so—you know my wife?

HILDE: I don't know her well, but yes—we were at that spa together for a few days.

SOLNESS: Oh—up *there*—

HILDE: Yes. And she told me I should be sure to pay a visit if I came to town. It was a sort of superfluous invitation, wasn't it?—ha ha ha—

SOLNESS: Hm—she certainly never mentioned anything of the sort to me . . .

HILDE: Well, I'm going to ask if I might be allowed to stay here tonight.

SOLNESS: Oh—well—I'm sure that could be—arranged— yes—

HILDE: Because I don't have any clothes here at all, apart from what I'm wearing. I mean, I've got some underwear in my things over there, but it's absolutely filthy!—ha ha ha— overdue for a wash!—ha ha—

SOLNESS: Ah—ergh—well—we can take care of that also, I'm sure . . . And—

DR. HERDAL: So! In the meantime, I'll do my house calls, and—

SOLNESS: Yes, exactly, and then you can come right back.

DR. HERDAL: I'll come right back!—you're goddamned right! Aha ha ha ha! Aha ha ha ha! I'll come right back!

(He goes out, and Solness calls to Mrs. Solness.)

SOLNESS: Aline! Would you be kind enough to come in here, please? There's a Miss Wangel here, whom you know, apparently.

MRS. SOLNESS *(Coming into the room)*: A Miss Who, did you say? *(Sees Hilde)* Oh! Is it—you? So! You did come to visit our town after all.

SOLNESS: Yes, Miss Wangel has just this very moment arrived in town, and so—she wondered if she might be able to stay here overnight . . .

MRS. SOLNESS: Here—at the house? Well—er—we'd be delighted.

SOLNESS: You know, so that she can get herself organized a bit and sort of—

MRS. SOLNESS *(To Hilde)*: Well, I'll certainly do my best to look after you . . . "An unexpected guest is a blessed obligation,"

my Aunt Thea used to say. So——mm——I suppose your luggage will be coming along later? . . .

HILDE: No, I——I don't have any.

MRS. SOLNESS: Oh! Well, that's all right. I'm sure it will all be
fine, anyway. *(A pause)* So! I'm afraid you'll have to be sat-
isfied with my husband's company for a little while. I'm
going to see about getting a room into some sort of shape
for you . . .

SOLNESS: Well, why don't we put Miss Wangel in one of the
children's rooms? They're already made up.

MRS. SOLNESS: Oh——yes, we certainly have plenty of space in
there . . .

*(She goes out. Hilde wanders around the room, looking at
things.)*

HILDE: Do you have many children's rooms——here in the
house?

SOLNESS: Yes, we have——three, altogether.

HILDE: Mmm——that's quite a few! So I suppose——you must
have quite a few children——?

SOLNESS: No. We don't have any children . . . But, in the meantime, *you* can be our child.

HILDE: Oh yes, I'll be your child——for tonight. But——I won't
cry, I'll try to see if I can sleep like a stone right through
the night.

SOLNESS: Yes, I'm sure you're bound to be awfully tired.

HILDE: No, not at all. But I do love to lie in bed——to sleep——and
dream . . .

SOLNESS: So, when you go to sleep at night——do you often dream?

HILDE: Oh yes——practically always!

SOLNESS: And what do you dream about most, then?

HILDE: Oh, I won't tell you that. Not tonight. I might tell you
some time.

(She wanders around for a while.)

SOLNESS: Are you—er—trying to find something?

HILDE: Oh no, I'm just looking at things— Should I—not do that?

SOLNESS: Oh no, go right ahead.

(She keeps looking. She picks something up from the table.)

HILDE: Are you the one who writes in this ledger?

SOLNESS: No. The—ah—the bookkeeper writes in that ledger.

HILDE: Oh, I see. And would that be—er—a member—of the other sex?—

SOLNESS: Yes—naturally—

HILDE: A person of that sex who's—regularly employed here?

SOLNESS: Yes.

HILDE: And is she perhaps—married?

SOLNESS: No—

HILDE: Aha!—I see . . .

SOLNESS: But she's going to be getting married very soon, I believe.

HILDE: Well, that's very nice for her, isn't it.

SOLNESS: Yes, it is, it is, but it's not so nice for me, because I'm going to be left with no one here to help me.

HILDE: But—can't you find someone else who'd be just as good?

SOLNESS: Well—perhaps *you* could stay here and write in the ledger.

HILDE: Oh, yes, can you imagine that? Ha ha ha—thank you very much, that is something that is never going to happen. Because I believe I might have some business to attend to here which has nothing to do with bookkeeping—am I right? Don't you agree?

SOLNESS: Oh—er—yes—absolutely . . . *(Pause)* I mean, the first thing you'll do, obviously, is to go around to the shops and get some proper clothes for yourself!—ha ha—

HILDE *(Cheerfully)*: No—I think I'm going to omit that step.

SOLNESS: Oh?

HILDE: Yes, because I'm afraid I've already spent all my money. Squandered it, unfortunately.

SOLNESS: So, then . . . It seems you have no luggage . . . No money . . . Ha ha ha—

HILDE: That's right! But—you know—what the hell, as they say!—aha ha ha ha—

SOLNESS: Whoa! Ha ha! My dear—you know—that attitude—really—makes me—like you.

HILDE: Oh—is that the only thing that does?

SOLNESS: Oh no, no, no. There are *many* things—ha ha ha . . . heh heh . . . *(A pause)* So. Tell me. Is your father still alive?

HILDE: Yes. He is . . .

SOLNESS: But you were thinking, maybe, that—mm—you'd like to come and study here in our town? . . .

HILDE: No, that's never occurred to me.

SOLNESS: So you're coming for a long visit? . . . Or . . . ?

HILDE: It all depends on how things develop, doesn't it? *(She takes a band out of her hair and places it on the table)* Master Builder Solness?

SOLNESS: Yes?

HILDE: Do you think you're a very—forgetful person?

SOLNESS: Forgetful? No. I'm not *aware* that I am.

(Pause.)

HILDE: But are you really not going to speak to me at all about what happened—up there?

SOLNESS: Up there—at Lysanger? Well, there isn't really very much to say about it, is there?

HILDE: Er—why are you talking like this?

SOLNESS: Well—tell me what you're referring to . . .

(A long silence. Then she begins.)

HILDE: All right. Well. When the tower on the old church was completed, we had a big celebration in town.

SOLNESS: Oh, I haven't forgotten that! I could never forget that extraordinary day . . .

HILDE: No? Well, it's so nice of you to say that.

(Silence again.)

So. There was music in the churchyard. And many, many hundreds of people. And all of us girls from the school were dressed in white, and we all had little flags.

SOLNESS: Oh yes, I remember those flags!

HILDE: And then *you* started to climb the tower. Right up the scaffolding! All the way up to the very highest point. And as you climbed, you were carrying an enormous wreath. And you hung that wreath all the way up on the weather vane where the—

SOLNESS *(Interrupting)*: Yes, I used to do that at that time, because that's a very old custom, you know—the Ceremony of the Wreath!

HILDE: It was so incredibly suspenseful and exciting to stand down there and watch you. "Just think!—oh!—imagine!—what if he were to fall? What if—the Master Builder—were to *fall*!?"

SOLNESS: Yes, well—yes, well, yes, it could have happened, actually. Because one of those little angels in white—one of those terrifying little evil devils—was screaming up at me—

HILDE: "Bravo Master Builder Solness!" Yes!

SOLNESS: —and she was waving her flag around so wildly that, when I saw it, something happened—I started to feel dizzy—I—

HILDE: Look. I was the devil who waved that flag . . .

SOLNESS: Yes—I see—it *was* you!

HILDE: I couldn't believe that there was a man on earth who could build such an incredibly high tower. And then that that very same man could stand there on top of it—and not even become the slightest bit dizzy—

SOLNESS: Well—er—

HILDE: And then—afterwards—that's when the—the thing happened, which—

SOLNESS: —which—what?—

HILDE: Well, I'm sure I don't have to remind you of *that* part of the story . . .

SOLNESS: I'm sorry. Please . . .

(A long pause.)

HILDE: Well, do you remember that a big banquet was held in your honor at the club?

SOLNESS: Oh yes—of course . . .

HILDE: Well, after the banquet, you were invited to come over to *our* house for tea.

SOLNESS: Why, that's absolutely right. Hm—I must say, Miss Wangel, it's really rather remarkable how well you've managed to remember all these meaningless details . . .

HILDE: "Meaningless details"? —Ha ha— You're really quite funny, aren't you? Ha ha ha— And do you think it was also a sort of "meaningless detail" that when you came into the living room *I* was there, completely alone?

SOLNESS: Oh—er—were you?

HILDE: I don't think you said I was an "evil devil" then.

SOLNESS: Well—ha ha—I'm sure I didn't . . .

HILDE: You said I was beautiful in my white dress. Beautiful. Like a very small princess, you said.

SOLNESS: I'm sure you did look like a princess, Miss Wangel.

HILDE: And then you said that, when I grew up, I would be *your* princess.

SOLNESS: Whoo—well! Did I say that, too? Heh heh heh—

HILDE: Yes. You did. And then when I asked you how long I would have to wait before you came back, you said you would return in ten years, and like some weird half-human mountain creature you would seize me and kidnap me, you would abduct me, and you would carry me away

33

to Spain or some strange place like that. And there, you
promised, you would buy me a kingdom.

SOLNESS: I would buy you a kingdom! Yes! Yes! Well of course
after a banquet, with all sorts of lovely things to eat and
drink—ha ha ha ha!—one never would think of buying
anything cheap!! Aha ha ha ha. But—oh my God—did
I really say all those things?

HILDE: Yes, you did. And you also said what my kingdom would
be called.

SOLNESS: Oh? Er—tell me!—

HILDE: The Kingdom of Orange Juice.

SOLNESS: Well—that sounds delicious! Ha ha ha—

HILDE: Well, I didn't like it. It was as if you were trying to
make fun of me . . .

SOLNESS: Well, I'm sure I had no desire to hurt your feelings—
I—

HILDE: No, I'm sure you *didn't*. I would imagine *not*. When you
think of what you were about to do . . .

SOLNESS: Er—what on earth was I about to do?

HILDE: You're saying now that you've forgotten that? Well,
that—that— No! No! Those are things that a person
remembers forever!

SOLNESS: Please. I'm sorry. I—

HILDE: You held me. And you kissed me—Master Builder Solness.

SOLNESS: I—I did?—

HILDE: Yes. You did. You held me, very tightly, you pressed yourself against me so hard that we leaned over backwards, and
you kissed me, you kissed me—again and again . . .

SOLNESS: No, but—but that's—

HILDE: No—you can't—you're not going to say you didn't do
that?!

SOLNESS: I absolutely—I—I did not do that!

(*Long silence. She stares at him with contempt and then
walks slowly away and stands in one position, not moving,
facing away from him.*)

Please—are you—?

(She is silent and motionless.)

Please, don't just—I— This—this story that you've told
me—it—it has to be something that you *dreamed*—very
vividly, maybe. It— Are you listening to me?

(He puts his hand on her arm. She pulls away roughly.)

All right—look—I—I—I must have been thinking about
it. I must have *wanted* it. I must have felt like doing it, and
the impression of that feeling was so strong that you—

(She remains as before. Then:)

Yes! Yes! All right! All right then! I did it!—it happened . . .

(A long silence.)

HILDE *(Moves a little bit without looking at him)*: So you admit
it now?
SOLNESS: Yes, yes—
HILDE: You took hold of me, and wrapped your arms tightly
around me?—
SOLNESS: Yes—
HILDE: —and then you pressed into me, hard, so that we bent
over backwards?—
SOLNESS: —yes—
HILDE: —and you were kissing me and kissing me, again and
again—
SOLNESS: Yes, that's right.
HILDE: So, you see, I've finally lured the little animal out of its
hole. I've brought it out of you.
SOLNESS: Yes, how strange—that I could forget something like
that . . .

HILDE: Well, I'm sure you've kissed so many girls in the course of your life—it's probably hard to remember them all . . .

SOLNESS: No, don't say that . . . But—er—

HILDE: Yes?

SOLNESS: Er—how did—I mean—what happened *then*—?

HILDE: *Nothing* happened, as you know very well, because all the other guests came into the room.

SOLNESS: Oh yes—that's right! . . . So incredible—that I could forget that, too! . . .

HILDE: Oh, you haven't actually forgotten any of it. You're just a little bit—a little bit embarrassed about what you did. People don't forget things like that. They just don't.

SOLNESS: Yes, it would seem—impossible, to forget things like that . . .

HILDE: Or *have* you perhaps forgotten *one* thing, anyway?— what *day* it was?

SOLNESS: What day it was?—

HILDE: Yes—what day it was—the day when you carried the wreath to the top of the tower—what was the day? Tell me! Say it!

SOLNESS: Well—ergh—God—I just—the actual day—I mean, I only know it was ten years ago—and well into the autumn—er—mm—

HILDE: Yes, it was ten years ago. It was September the nineteenth.

SOLNESS: Why yes, that's right, it *was* around then— Goodness—so—you remember that too! Ha ha ha— *(Stops)* But wait a minute! —What?—ha ha—heh heh heh—it's September the nineteenth *today*—isn't it?—

HILDE: Yes, it's September the nineteenth. And the ten years are up. And you didn't come—as you promised you would.

SOLNESS: Promised—?—ha ha—oh yes, I threatened to come get you, didn't I? Ha ha ha—

HILDE: I didn't see it as a threat.

SOLNESS: Well, you know, a teasing sort of threat . . .

HILDE: Oh, was that what you were doing? Were you teasing me?

SOLNESS: Well, I was joking around—you know—I was having a little fun with you—I mean, Jesus Christ, I don't know, I don't *remember*, but that's all it could possibly have been, because you were only a *child*—I mean, Jesus *Christ*!

HILDE: Oh I don't know how much of a *child* I was. I wasn't exactly the innocent little girl you might think I was . . .

SOLNESS: But what are you saying? Are you saying that for ten years you've seriously been expecting that I would return to Lysanger?

HILDE: Well, yes, of course. That's exactly what I expected.

SOLNESS: That I would come to your house and—and carry you away with me?

HILDE: Yes—like a weird, half-human mountain creature.

SOLNESS: And that I would make you—my—my princess? . . .

HILDE: That's what you promised me.

SOLNESS: And that I would—give you a—a kingdom?

HILDE: Well—why not? It didn't have to be the ordinary *kind* of kingdom . . .

SOLNESS: Just simply something that was—just as nice as one? . . .

HILDE: Yes, something that was just as nice—or maybe nicer! After all—if you could build the highest church tower in the world, then surely you could find some way of creating—a special sort of—kingdom . . .

(A silence.)

SOLNESS: You know, honestly, I can't figure you out at all . . .

HILDE: Really? You can't? But I'm so simple! At least *I* think I am.

SOLNESS: Well, you're not so simple, because I honestly can't tell whether you really mean all these things you're saying or whether you're joking.

HILDE: Oh—you mean—teasing you? The way you teased me?—ha ha ha—

SOLNESS: And by the way, haven't you known for all this time that I happen to be married?

HILDE: Yes. Of course. Why do you ask that?

SOLNESS: Oh, I don't know. I just . . . Look. Tell me honestly. Why have you come here?

HILDE: Why? Why? I've come to take over my kingdom. The time is up now. Bring me my kingdom, Master Builder! Now! Now!

SOLNESS: No, seriously. Tell me. Why *have* you come? What do you actually want to do here?

HILDE: What do I want to do? Well, first, before anything, I so much want to make a little tour of all the buildings you've built around here.

SOLNESS: Oh—well! Then you're going to have a lot of running around to do!

HILDE: Yes, you've done such an enormous amount of work.

SOLNESS: Well, I have, really, especially in these last few years.

HILDE: Have you done a lot of church towers?—those really high ones?

SOLNESS: No. I don't do those anymore.

HILDE: Well, what do you do, then?

SOLNESS: I build homes. You know—for human beings—ha ha—

HILDE: Hm. I wonder: wouldn't it be possible to build something like church towers—on people's homes?

SOLNESS: My God—you know, it's remarkable that you say that, because that's exactly what I'd *like* to do more than anything in the world . . .

HILDE: Well, why don't you do it, then?

SOLNESS: Because people don't want it!

HILDE: But that's unbelievable! They don't want it? That's just incredible!

SOLNESS: But just now, you see, I'm actually building a new home for Aline and myself, just in front here . . .

HILDE: Really . . .

SOLNESS: Yes, it's almost finished. And on top of *this* home there *is* a tower.

HILDE: A high one?

SOLNESS: Oh yes.

HILDE: A *very* high one?

SOLNESS: Well, believe me—the people around here are going to say that it's much *too* high. Oh, *much* too high for a person's home!—ha ha ha—

(A long silence.)

Er—so—er—Miss Wangel, tell me—what's your first name?

(A pause.)

HILDE: Hilde. It's Hilde.

SOLNESS: Oh—Hilde! Really!

HILDE: You don't remember that my name is Hilde? You certainly called me that ten years ago . . .

SOLNESS: I did, eh?

HILDE: Actually you called me "little Hilde." And that I *didn't* like.

SOLNESS: No? You didn't? You didn't like it that I called you "little Hilde"?

HILDE: No, I didn't. But in any case, now—well, I quite like the sound of "Princess Hilde." Yes, I think that will do from now on.

SOLNESS: Yes, exactly. Princess Hilde—of—of—what was that kingdom going to be called? . . .

HILDE: No, no. I'm sick of that kingdom! I don't want that kingdom—I want a different one now!

SOLNESS: Ha ha ha— *(A pause)* Look, it's—it's very very good for me that you came to me now, at this particular moment.

HILDE *(Looks deeply into his eyes)*: It is? Really?

SOLNESS: Yes. Because I've just been sitting here in this house— I've been sitting here with a feeling of being completely alone . . . I've been sitting here just staring helplessly at—

at everything around me . . . And you know, the funny thing is that I've become so disturbed by younger people!

HILDE: What? Younger people? . . .

SOLNESS: Yes, they upset me so much that I've sort of closed my door here and locked myself in. Because I'm afraid they're going to come here, and they're going to knock on the door, and then they're going to break in.

HILDE: Well, I think maybe you should open the door and *let* them in.

SOLNESS: Open the door?

HILDE: Yes—so that they can just gently and quietly come inside, and it can be something good for you . . .

SOLNESS: Open the door? . . .

(Hilde looks at him.)

HILDE *(With a quivering twitch around her mouth, she asks him)*: Can you—Master Builder—can you—in some way—make use of me?

(Before he can answer, Dr. Herdal comes in.)

DR. HERDAL: Well!—are you two still talking?

SOLNESS: Oh yes—the two of us have had quite a bit to talk about . . .

HILDE: Oh it's been wonderfully interesting. Because Master Builder Solness has such an absolutely incredible memory! I mean, he instantly recalls even the most meaningless details . . .

(Mrs. Solness comes in.)

MRS. SOLNESS: Well, Miss Wangel, the room is all ready for you now.

HILDE: Oh—you're being so kind to me.

SOLNESS: One of the children's rooms?

MRS. SOLNESS: Yes—the middle one. But first—we should probably have something to eat.

(A silence.)

SOLNESS: So Hilde will sleep in one of the children's rooms . . .

MRS. SOLNESS: "Hilde"?

SOLNESS: Yes—Miss Wangel—is called Hilde. And do you know?—I knew Hilde when she was a child!

MRS. SOLNESS: You did?! Well! Halvard! Really! *(A pause)* Well then—supper is ready. *(She escorts Dr. Herdal off)*

SOLNESS: Hilde—for all these years—there's been a person— someone—whom I've been longing for, whom I've needed, whom I've missed—desperately, painfully—I know that was you.

HILDE *(Looks at him, her eyes full of wonder and joy)*: The world is beautiful.

SOLNESS: Yes?

HILDE: I have my kingdom!

SOLNESS: Hilde!—

HILDE *(Once more with that quivering twitch around her mouth)*: I meant—I almost have it. I should have said— "almost" . . .

(She goes out. The lights begin to fade. Solness speaks to the audience.)

SOLNESS: And then we all go in and have a very nice dinner.

(The lights get quite dim, and then they slowly get quite bright.)

And the next morning, the sky is blue, and the sun is shining.

(There is a table with plants on it. Mrs. Solness comes in and tends to them. Solness slowly looks through the large portfo-

lio which contains Ragnar's drawings. After a while, Kaya comes in. She seems to be about to speak to Solness but turns instead to the audience.)

KAYA *(To the audience)*: Let's take fifteen minutes.

(Intermission.)

PART TWO

Mrs. Solness tending the plants, Solness looking at Ragnar's drawings, as before. Kaya comes in.

KAYA *(To Solness)*: Hello. I just wanted to say that I'm here.

SOLNESS: Good. Good.

(A silence.)

How's Old Brovik doing today?

KAYA: Mm—not too well. He said to tell you he's terribly sorry, but he has to spend the day in bed.

SOLNESS: Of course, of course. He *must* stay in bed. Well, you can get to work, if you like.

KAYA: I'll see you later. *(She goes out)*

MRS. SOLNESS: Yes, the *next* one to die. So he's on his way, too.

SOLNESS: He's on his way, too? What's that supposed to mean?

MRS. SOLNESS: Old Brovik—oh yes, he's *certainly* going to die. Oh yes—we'll be hearing of his death very soon now, I'd say.

43

SOLNESS: Aline—darling—do you think maybe you should go out for a while and take a little walk or something?

MRS. SOLNESS: Oh absolutely, yes, that is exactly the thing that I need to do! *(She continues to tend to the plants as before)*

SOLNESS: Is she—er—still asleep?

MRS. SOLNESS: Oh, you're wondering about—Miss Wangel?

SOLNESS: Yes, I just suddenly wondered about her . . .

MRS. SOLNESS: Well, Miss Wangel has actually been up for hours.

SOLNESS: Oh! Really?

MRS. SOLNESS: Yes, when I went to look in on her, she was busy arranging all of her things.

SOLNESS: So—we've finally found a good use for one of the children's rooms, haven't we, Aline?

MRS. SOLNESS: Yes. At last.

SOLNESS: It's so wonderful to not just leave all of them empty . . .

MRS. SOLNESS: Yes, the nightmare of that—emptiness . . . You're quite right, Halvard.

SOLNESS: Things—are going to be better, my darling. Believe me, things are going to start to get better. Everything's going to be easier and nicer for both of us. Particularly for you—I—

MRS. SOLNESS: Things are going to start to get better?

SOLNESS: Believe me, Aline—

MRS. SOLNESS: You mean—because—that girl has come here?—

SOLNESS: No—no—I meant—you know—now that we're going to move into our new house . . .

MRS. SOLNESS: Ah. Do you believe that, Halvard? Do you really believe that will make things better?

SOLNESS: I don't doubt it for a second. I mean, you think that, too—don't you?

MRS. SOLNESS: No, because when I think about the new house, I just—go blank—I feel absolutely nothing.

SOLNESS: You know, it's very, very hard for me, Aline, to hear you say that. Because you're the main reason—I mean, I built it for you!

MRS. SOLNESS: Yes—for me. Yes, you do much too much "for me."

SOLNESS: I mean, I'm telling you that it's terribly, terribly hurtful when you say things like that. It's almost more than I can stand. It's as if you're stabbing me with a knife when you say things like that!

MRS. SOLNESS: Well—then I just won't say them.

SOLNESS: And I still have to tell you: you're going to see that I'm right—things *are* going to be nice, things are going to be very very nice for you, Aline, when we move into the new house!

MRS. SOLNESS: Oh my God—nice for me—

SOLNESS: Yes! Yes! They will be! Because there's going to be so much there that's going to remind you of your own—

MRS. SOLNESS: Oh, that's going to remind me of my parents' house? That's going to remind me of my parents' house that burned down in the fire?

SOLNESS: Aline—darling—

MRS. SOLNESS: Don't you understand? You can work and build for the rest of your life, Halvard, but you'll never be able to give me back a home that really feels right to me!

SOLNESS: Well then for God's sake let's not talk anymore about this subject.

MRS. SOLNESS: Oh well, we never do talk about it anyway. You know, you avoid the subject anyway.

SOLNESS: I *avoid* the *subject*? I *avoid* the *subject*? Why in the world would I do that?

MRS. SOLNESS: Oh, Halvard, I know you so well. You really would like to save me from everything that weighs down on me. And you want to pardon me, too, my dear Halvard. As much as you possibly can.

SOLNESS: *Pardon?* Pardon *you*? What do you mean, pardon *you*?

MRS. SOLNESS: Of course, me. Of *course* me. *I know that.*

SOLNESS: Oh my God—this again?

MRS. SOLNESS: Because with my parents' house—yes, all right, whatever was going to happen was going to happen—

when terrible things start to fall out of the sky, you can't stop them . . .

SOLNESS: Of course, of course . . .

MRS. SOLNESS: But the horror—what happened after the fire—*that's* the thing—*that—that—that—*

SOLNESS: Aline!—you can't—don't *think* about that . . .

MRS. SOLNESS: But yes, *that's* the thing I *have* to think about, and I'm even going to get to *speak* about it now, for once, because the pain is unbearable, and it's the one thing I will never have the right to forgive myself for.

SOLNESS: To *forgive*—?

MRS. SOLNESS: Yes—yes—because I had responsibilities. In both directions. To you—*and* to the children. And I should have forced myself to be strong. I shouldn't have allowed my fear to completely overpower me. I shouldn't have allowed my grief—my grief that my home was burned down in front of me—If only I could have done it, Halvard—

SOLNESS: Aline, you have to promise me that you will never start thinking like this again . . . You have to promise—

MRS. SOLNESS: Oh God, Jesus—promise! Promise! You can promise all you like—

SOLNESS: Oh God, it's so hopeless. There's never a ray of light. There's never a ray of light. Never even one ray of light inside this home we live in . . .

MRS. SOLNESS: Halvard, please, this isn't a home.

SOLNESS: Ah. All right. Fine. It isn't. And I don't know, you may well be right that things won't be better in the new house—I just—

MRS. SOLNESS: No—no—it's going to be just as empty . . . completely deserted . . .

SOLNESS: But then why in the world have we built it then? Can you explain that to me?

MRS. SOLNESS: I'm afraid you'll have to answer that question yourself.

SOLNESS *(Suspiciously)*: What? What does that mean? What are you trying to say to me, Aline?

MRS. SOLNESS: What am I trying to say?

SOLNESS: Yes, goddammit! I think you were speaking very strangely there, as if you were thinking certain little thoughts to yourself—

MRS. SOLNESS: I can assure you I wasn't.

SOLNESS: Look, I know what I know! I happen to still have extremely good eyesight and extremely good hearing, and I think you should keep that very much in mind, Aline!—

MRS. SOLNESS: What are you talking about? Are you talking about something?

SOLNESS: Aline, let's be serious—do you think you might just possibly be going around here looking to see if there's a special hidden significance in the things I do and the things I say?

MRS. SOLNESS: The—what? Am I—*what?*

SOLNESS: Ha ha ha ha! Ha ha ha! Well, it's totally understandable, Aline, it really is—how else could you behave when you're forced to cope with a mentally sick man in the house?—aha ha ha—

MRS. SOLNESS: Mentally sick? Are you mentally sick?

SOLNESS: Well, let's not say "sick"—let's say a bit "disturbed," a bit "unbalanced"—

MRS. SOLNESS: Halvard—for Christ in Heaven's sake—

SOLNESS: But oddly, you're mistaken. You and Doctor Herdal are both completely mistaken, because I'm not actually suffering from anything of the kind. As a matter of fact, there's absolutely nothing wrong with me.

MRS. SOLNESS: Well of course there isn't! But what are you so upset about, then?

SOLNESS: Upset? Am I upset? Well, I think I might be upset because of the burden of all the guilt, Aline.

MRS. SOLNESS: But—but you have no reason to feel guilty towards anyone.

SOLNESS: Oh, well—towards you, Aline. You know, it's pretty hard to measure, because it's infinite . . . infinite . . .

MRS. SOLNESS: What's behind all this, Halvard? You might as
well tell me.

SOLNESS: But there *isn't* anything! Goddammit! I haven't done
anything! I haven't! And yet I feel I'm being crushed, I'm
being ground down into the dirt, overpowered by guilt . . .

MRS. SOLNESS: Towards me?

SOLNESS: Yes, towards you, my dear.

MRS. SOLNESS: Then you really *are* sick. You are, Halvard.

SOLNESS: I suppose I must be. Or something of that nature.

(They see Hilde approaching them.)

Well! That brings in a little light, now, doesn't it, Aline?

HILDE: Good morning, Master Builder.

SOLNESS: Did you sleep well?

HILDE: It was wonderful! As if I were being rocked in a cradle.
I just lay there and stretched out like—a princess!

SOLNESS: Very appropriate . . . And did you *dream* a little bit
too, maybe?

HILDE: Yes—but that was awful.

SOLNESS: Oh?

HILDE: I dreamt I was falling down an enormously high, steep
cliff. Do you ever have that dream?

SOLNESS: Yes, sometimes I do . . .

HILDE: It's horrible, but it's an exciting feeling—the way you
sort of drift down, farther and farther—

SOLNESS: —and there's a sort of *icy* sensation, isn't there?—
cold—freezing—

HILDE: Yes!—And do you sometimes pull your legs up under
you—as you fall? . . .

SOLNESS: Yes, right up to my chest . . .

HILDE: Yes! Yes!

MRS. SOLNESS: Well!—er—Halvard—I suppose I'd better go
on to town now. *(To Hilde)* I'll see if I can find a few
clothes and things that you're obviously going to need—

HILDE: Oh dear, lovely Mrs. Solness! That is so incredibly kind of you! You're so kind!

MRS. SOLNESS: It's one's simple obligation to a guest, my dear. I'm not kind at all.

HILDE *(Somewhat upset)*: Well, but I mean, I can perfectly well go to town myself and get what I need. Or maybe you don't think that's a good idea.

MRS. SOLNESS: To be absolutely frank, I think you might possibly attract attention there, somehow.

HILDE: Oh really? Attention? Hee hee—that would be fun!—wouldn't it?—hee hee hee—

SOLNESS: Yes, but then the people there might start to think that you too were crazy . . .

HILDE: Crazy? Why? Are there an enormous number of crazy people here in your town?

SOLNESS *(Pointing to his forehead)*: Well, there's *one* at least.

HILDE: You—Master Builder?—

MRS. SOLNESS: Oh *God*—will you stop this, *please*?

SOLNESS *(To Hilde)*: What? You mean—you haven't noticed it yet?

HILDE: No—not at all—I absolutely—mm— *(Thinks twice and laughs a little)* Well, I mean, maybe, you know, in one particular way—aha ha ha—

SOLNESS: Oho! Do you hear that, Aline?

MRS. SOLNESS: What *is* that one particular way, then, Miss Wangel? Tell us.

HILDE: No, no, I'm not going to say.

SOLNESS: Oh come on, tell us!

HILDE: No thanks! Do you think *I'm* crazy? Ha ha ha ha ha! Ha ha ha ha ha!

MRS. SOLNESS: When you and Miss Wangel are alone, Halvard, I'm sure she'll tell you.

SOLNESS: Really? Do you think so?

MRS. SOLNESS: Oh yes, because you knew her so well at one time—when she was a child—you told me . . .

(Mrs. Solness goes out. A pause.)

HILDE: So. Is your wife just incapable of liking me at all?

SOLNESS: I'm sorry—I—

HILDE: I mean—

SOLNESS: It's— In these last few years—Aline's become very reclusive—ill at ease around people—

HILDE: Yes? . . .

SOLNESS: If you could only get to know her a little . . . You see, she's actually a kind, good, wonderful person . . .

HILDE: Well, if she's really so kind, why did she talk that way about "obligation"?

SOLNESS: "Obligation"?

HILDE: Yes—she said she was going to go out and buy some things for me—out of *obligation.* Christ, I *hate* that word—it's so revolting, so ugly—

SOLNESS: "Obligation"?—

HILDE: It sounds like someone being strangled to death. —"Obligation!" "Obligation!" Don't you hear it? Someone being *strangled* . . .

SOLNESS: Well—I've—

HILDE: And if she's really so kind—as you say she is—why would she use a word like that?

SOLNESS: Well, but what sort of words do you think she should have used?

HILDE: She might have said that she wanted to buy me some things because she liked me very much and she wanted to do it. That's what she could have said. Something warm, from her heart. Don't you understand what I'm talking about?

SOLNESS: That's what you hoped that Aline would say?

HILDE: Yes, it is.

(She walks around the room, picks up Ragnar's portfolio.)

Are you the one who's done all these drawings?

50

SOLNESS: No—they were done by a young man whom I have here assisting me.

HILDE: Oh—someone you've trained?

SOLNESS: Yes . . .

HILDE *(Looking carefully at the drawings)*: An advanced practitioner . . . *(She keeps looking)*

SOLNESS: Do you think you can tell that from looking at those drawings?

HILDE: *No*—I meant that if he's studied with *you*, then he must be a very—

SOLNESS: Oh no, believe me, there are a lot of people around here who have studied with me, and they haven't advanced very far at all!—aha ha ha!

HILDE: But why do you take on all these students? I don't understand.

SOLNESS: Well, it's—

HILDE: I think it's absurd. You shouldn't teach students the things you know, because *you're* the only one who should be allowed to build! You should get all the jobs yourself.

SOLNESS: Hilde—!

HILDE: What?

SOLNESS: Ha ha ha ha! Hilde! That's outrageous! Ha ha ha—

(Her attention is caught by something she sees through a window. She studies it.)

HILDE: Over there . . . *(He goes to her)*

SOLNESS: Where? By the stone quarry?

HILDE: Yes. Is that your new house?

SOLNESS: Yes.

HILDE: It's so big.

SOLNESS: Yes . . .

HILDE: So does that one have children's rooms also?

SOLNESS: Yes, it does.

HILDE: Hm. Children's rooms. But no children . . .

SOLNESS: Yes.

HILDE *(With a half smile)*: Well, then wasn't I possibly just a little bit right?

SOLNESS: What do you mean?

HILDE: I mean, that you really are—just a little bit—crazy?

SOLNESS: Was that what you had in mind when you said that?

HILDE: Yes—I was thinking about all your empty children's rooms . . .

(A pause.)

SOLNESS: Hilde, Aline and I did have—children . . .

HILDE: Oh . . .

SOLNESS: Two little boys—twins . . . It was ten or eleven years ago . . .

HILDE: And they're both?—mm—

SOLNESS: We only had them for—a little less than three weeks. And then, they died . . . Oh Hilde, it's so good for me—so unbelievably good for me that you came here. It's such a wonderful feeling to have someone to talk with . . .

HILDE: So—you mean—you can't talk with her?

SOLNESS: No. Not in the way I want to talk—and need to talk. We simply can't talk about this. Or about—most things, really . . .

HILDE: So—was that what you meant yesterday when you said that you needed me? Was that the only thing? Or—

SOLNESS: Hilde—please—I don't know. I don't know any-more—I'm not sure—I— *(Breaking off)* Just sit with me, Hilde. Please. Right here . . . Would you like to—hear about it?

HILDE: Yes. Please. Yes.

SOLNESS: I'll tell you everything, then.

(They look out toward the new house.)

You see, over there, on the high ground—where you can see the new house—

HILDE: Yes?—

SOLNESS: That was where Aline and I lived when we were first married. Because at that time there was an old house there which had belonged to her mother. And that house had been given to us, along with this whole enormous garden around it.

HILDE: And did that house also have—a tower?

SOLNESS: Oh no—nothing like that. In fact, from the outside that house was honestly just a huge, dark, depressing, ugly *box*. Inside, though, it was actually quite comfortable and cozy. And that was where we lived when the two little boys were born. And do you know?—when they came into the world, they were so healthy and strong—they were growing every day—you could actually *see* it!—

HILDE: Yes, they grow so fast in the very first days—

SOLNESS: —and the sight of Aline, lying in bed with the two little babies—well, that was the most beautiful sight you could ever see in your life. But then—one night—we had a fire—

HILDE: A fire? What happened?

SOLNESS: Well, that was a terrible night—alarms, chaos— everyone scrambling and pushing, outside in the dark in the freezing cold, Aline and the boys carried out in their beds—well, Aline went into a state of sheer terror, and as a result she developed a fever. And that, as it turned out, affected her milk. She insisted that she had to nurse the little babies herself, no matter how ill she was, she felt it was her obligation. And so—both boys got sick—and both died.

HILDE: They couldn't survive drinking the milk . . .

SOLNESS: No—that's right.

HILDE: That must have been so hard for you—so painful—

SOLNESS: Yes. And it was ten times worse for Aline . . . Think about it—can you believe that things like that are allowed to happen in the world? From the day I lost my boys, I hated building churches. And so now I don't build churches anymore . . .

HILDE: Only homes. Where people can live . . .

SOLNESS: Yes—homes. For people.

HILDE: Homes with high towers and spires, though!

SOLNESS: Yes, I must admit I do prefer them that way . . . Well, anyway, you see, that fire lifted me up to a great height as a Master Builder. Because I parceled out almost that whole piece of land into lots for houses, and so then of course *I* was the one who could *build* the houses. And after that, everything started going in my direction.

HILDE: You must be a very happy man, the way it's all gone for you.

SOLNESS: Ah—so now you're saying that, too, like everybody else.

HILDE: Well—you must be. I think you must be. If you could only manage to stop thinking all the time about the two little children—

SOLNESS: Well—Hilde—

HILDE: I mean, do they still—stand in the way—of every-thing—all the time? After all these years?

SOLNESS: Listen to me—Hilde . . . when I told you just now about the fire—

HILDE: Yes?

SOLNESS: Well—when I told you what happened, wasn't there a certain rather obvious point that sort of sprang out at you? I mean that because of the fire I fell into a situation in which I was able to build these homes for people: com-fortable, bright, cozy homes, in which a mother, a father, and a whole group of children could live—in which they could live with the secure feeling, with the *wonderful* feel-ing, that it's a happy destiny simply to be alive, to be alive on this earth!—and even to have the feeling that the very best thing *in* life is to be together, to belong to one another, through all of life's many events . . .

HILDE: Well, doesn't that make you awfully happy?—that you can create such lovely homes for these people?

SOLNESS: But Hilde—don't you see that in order to get this opportunity to build homes for other people, I had to give up—forever—any hope at all of—of having a home myself? I mean, a home with a father and a mother and—children?

HILDE: You mean—you mean, because . . .

SOLNESS: That's the price I had to pay for what I received, for the wonderful good luck that people love to talk about. The price wasn't any cheaper than that, Hilde! And that was just the down payment!

HILDE: But couldn't—something good—still—happen? . . .

SOLNESS: No, no. No—that was one of the consequences of Aline's illness—the illness that was caused by the fire!

HILDE *(After a moment, looking deep into his eyes)*: And yet you're building a house with—rooms—for children . . .

SOLNESS: Hilde. Have you ever noticed that sometimes the thing which is *impossible* can somehow still tempt you, can somehow still cry out to you—?

HILDE: Yes! Yes! So you know about that too, do you?

SOLNESS: Yes, Hilde. I do.

HILDE: You sound like there might be a weird half-human creature running around somewhere inside you . . .

SOLNESS: Yes, maybe. *(Grimly)* But at any rate, there's a certain balancing that always occurs. In other words, everything I've done, everything I've achieved—it all has to be balanced out! And even after the down payment, a price must still be paid. And the currency in which the payment is demanded is not money—it's human happiness. And my good fortune can't be paid for with my *own* happiness alone—no, it also has to be paid for with the happiness of *other people*. And the price must be paid! And every single day of my life I have to get up and watch that price being paid, for my benefit, all day long. Paid and paid and paid and paid.

HILDE: So obviously you're talking about—your wife . . .

SOLNESS: Yes. Because you see, Aline had a vocation, just as I had. But her vocation had to be blocked, destroyed, it had to be ground down into a million pieces, so that mine could be advanced, so that I could obtain some sort of fabulous success. Because you have to understand this, Hilde— Aline also had a great talent. She had a talent for building and shaping the souls of young children. She would have enabled her children to grow up with a kind of equanimity and a kind of grace . . . She was born to be a shaper of souls, someone who would guide souls so that they could rise up out of childhood into noble and beautiful forms. And all of that talent just lies there now like a pile of rubble after an enormous explosion—it's completely useless.

HILDE: Yes, but—but even if all that is *true*, I—

SOLNESS: It *is* true. It *is* true. I *know* Aline. I *know*—

HILDE: Yes, but the point is, it wasn't your fault! None of it was your fault!

SOLNESS: Oh no? Well, that's the question, isn't it? Because I think that it probably *was* my fault.

HILDE: What? The fire?

SOLNESS: Yes. All of it. Everything that happened . . . But you know—I mean—well—maybe it wasn't my fault at all . . .

HILDE: Oh Master Builder—when you talk like that—you seem as if you really *are* mentally sick . . .

SOLNESS: Yes—well—

(Ragnar comes in, cautiously.)

RAGNAR: Oh—excuse me—

SOLNESS: No, no, please stay, so we can settle this finally.

RAGNAR: Yes. That would be great.

SOLNESS: Things aren't going any better for your father, I hear.

RAGNAR: No, he's deteriorating—very fast . . . That's why I've come here—to ask you—please—could you possibly write a few words on one of my drawings?—just anything that he could read before he—

SOLNESS: Ragnar—please—could you please stop talking to me about those drawings?

RAGNAR: Why? Have you looked at them?

SOLNESS: Yes—of course.

RAGNAR: So—perhaps you didn't find them—very—good? Or perhaps you don't think that *I* am—

SOLNESS: Ragnar, please just stay here and keep on working with me! You'll have everything you could possibly want. You can get married to Kaya. You'll live without any anxieties—you might even be happy! You just have to stop thinking about becoming a builder yourself!

RAGNAR: All right, fine. So that's what I'm going to be able to go home and tell Father. Fine. Good. Because I promised to tell him exactly what you said. And that's what you'd like me to tell him before he dies—right?

SOLNESS: Well, tell him—tell him whatever you like, for Christ's sake! The best thing, really, would be to tell him nothing! *(Suddenly exclaiming)* I can't act any differently from the way I act, Ragnar!

RAGNAR: May I take the drawings away with me, then?

SOLNESS: Yes—please—just—

HILDE: No—leave them.

SOLNESS: The—leave them for what?

HILDE: Well, because *I* want to look at them, too.

SOLNESS: But you already *have*. You— *(To Ragnar)* Fine— leave them . . . Ragnar! You mustn't ask me for something that I can't give you! Please, Ragnar, you mustn't do that!

RAGNAR: Hm—of course. Of course. Excuse me. *(He goes out)*

HILDE: That was—incredibly—cruel—I—

SOLNESS: Oh, you think so? Yes, that's what *he* was thinking.

HILDE: You were brutal with him—it was sickening—I—

SOLNESS: But you don't understand my situation!

HILDE: I don't care what your situation is—you shouldn't behave like that!

SOLNESS: You said I ought to be the only person allowed to build . . .

HILDE: Yes, I said it. But you shouldn't say it!

SOLNESS: For God's sake, Hilde, if I can't have a single moment of inner peace in my life, at least allow me to keep my position in the world!

HILDE: But why can't you have a single moment of inner peace?

SOLNESS: *Why?* Oh my God, Hilde, I . . .

HILDE: What? Tell me!

SOLNESS: All right. I'll tell you . . . But you see, it all begins with something so silly that it almost seems funny. I mean, the whole thing is all about a crack in a chimney pipe . . .

HILDE: Well—

SOLNESS: Yes, you see, in the old house where we used to live, the one that burned down—well, that house had an attic—and I used to go up there very frequently . . .

HILDE *(Impatiently)*: Yes—all right . . .

SOLNESS: Well, one day, long before the fire, I noticed a crack in the chimney pipe there. And every time I went up to the attic, I'd check to see if the crack was still there.

HILDE: And it always was . . .

SOLNESS: Well, yes—because no one but me knew about it.

HILDE: And you never mentioned it to anyone?

SOLNESS: No, I didn't.

HILDE: But a cracked chimney pipe is incredibly dangerous! Didn't it occur to you to get it fixed?

SOLNESS: Yes, of course—but each time I started to do something about it, something stopped me, as if a hand had suddenly appeared out of nowhere and was holding on to me. And I'd just say to myself, Well, I'll do it tomorrow. And so the crack was never mended.

HILDE: You just ignored it? How could you do that?

SOLNESS: Because I kept on wondering about that crack in the pipe: could I just possibly fly through that crack and fly up to a very great height—as a Master Builder?

HILDE: That must have been an exciting thought.

SOLNESS: I kept imagining this little story—and it seemed so natural, so simple and easy . . . Well, it would all take place, naturally, in wintertime. Just a little before lunch. And Aline and I would be out, and I'd be driving her around somewhere. And those who stayed behind would have lit big roaring fires in all of the stoves—

HILDE: Oh yes, because it would have been a terribly cold day . . .

SOLNESS: Yes, yes, bitterly cold—and of course the servants would have wanted the house to be nice and warm for when Aline would come in—

HILDE: Yes, because they would know that Aline simply always felt cold—

SOLNESS: Yes, she always did. And so it would happen—that as we would be riding towards home—we'd see smoke rising . . .

HILDE: You'd just see smoke?

SOLNESS: Yes, at first. But then, when we would reach the garden gate, we'd be able to see the whole house, like a big wooden box, in a ring of flame, a surging, pulsing ring of flame . . . That was my fantasy . . .

HILDE: Yes, I see. But seriously, tell me—are you absolutely certain that the fire was caused by that little crack in the chimney pipe?

SOLNESS: No, no, on the contrary. I know for a fact that the crack in the chimney pipe had absolutely nothing to do with it.

HILDE: What?—

SOLNESS: No, it was clearly determined that the fire broke out in a clothes closet in a completely different part of the house.

HILDE: Well then why are you talking to me about—?

SOLNESS: Hilde, please—please listen to me. I *will* explain this! You see, I have to ask you— Would you agree with me, possibly, that there are certain people in the world, certain particular "selected" individuals, who have received a certain—favor and—and been granted a certain power, so that they can desire something so passionately that the thing they wish for simply has to take place? Would you agree with me that there are such people?

HILDE: Well, *if* there are, we'll learn one day whether I am one of them.

SOLNESS: But Hilde, an individual can't accomplish things like that entirely on his own. No—there are forces in the universe that help people, that *serve* people, and in order for one's desires to be realized, those forces have to be there. But you see, they don't just suddenly appear, Hilde! One has to call for them, you see, with a sort of intense inner determination . . . And I did that. I called for them. I called, they came, and they did exactly what I wanted them to do. And that's why I say that it was my fault that the boys died and that Aline was never able to be what she should have been . . . You know, everyone says that I must be a very happy man, because I've been so terribly fortunate. But do you know what all that good fortune actually feels like? It feels like my skin has been peeled off, and there's a huge wound right about here in my chest, and it's still bleeding. And all the forces in the universe that help people and serve them—they're all flying out into the world on my behalf, and they're ripping the skin off more and more people, and they're bringing the skin back to me and trying to graft it on to my wound, but the graft won't take, and the wound won't heal. It won't heal! It will never heal . . .

HILDE *(Observes him carefully)*: You *are* sick, Master Builder. Maybe—almost—terribly sick.

SOLNESS: Say "crazy," Hilde, because that's what you mean.

HILDE: No—no—that's not right! Because look, you can reason, you can think, you can understand things—

SOLNESS: Well why am I sick then? Tell me. Tell me!

HILDE: I wonder if perhaps you were simply born with an oversensitive—an oversensitive—mm—*conscience*—yes . . .

SOLNESS: What in the world does *that* mean?

HILDE: I mean that your conscience is very delicate, Master Builder. It's much too weak! It's too easily crushed by heavy things . . .

SOLNESS: Is that right? Well then what sort of a conscience *should* I have?

HILDE: I'd like you to have a more robust conscience, Master Builder, which could lift *up* those heavy things and bear their weight . . .

SOLNESS: Aha—I see. And do *you*, perhaps, have a conscience like that?

HILDE: Mm—yes—I probably do . . .

SOLNESS: But has it really been put to the test? . . .

HILDE: Well, it was not an easy thing to leave my father, whom I love very dearly . . .

SOLNESS: Well, Hilde, to leave your father for a month or two is not—

HILDE: No—no—I won't ever go back.

SOLNESS: Oh! Really . . .

HILDE: You see, some power inside me drove me here—drove me, forced me . . . And I was pulled here too—pulled—drawn . . .

SOLNESS: Yes! That's right! That's it, Hilde! You see? You see? You're just like me. One of those weird half-human mountain creatures is living somewhere inside of you, too. Because they're the ones who call out—to the forces outside us . . . And when those forces come to you and hold on to you, you don't have any choice anymore—you have to surrender! . . . Oh, Hilde, Hilde, all around us—everywhere—*there are spirits*—and there really are spirits of light, and there really are spirits of darkness . . . If only—if only one could be sure whether it was a spirit of light or a spirit of darkness which was reaching out for us and holding on to us—then life could be better, Hilde . . .

HILDE: Yes, and life could also be better if one could have a truly healthy, truly robust conscience, so that one dared to do the things one really wanted to do!

(A long silence. He moves away from her.)

SOLNESS: Mm—I suppose most people are probably just as weak and pitiful as I am in *that* regard.

HILDE: Yes, they probably are . . .

SOLNESS: You know, in all the old books of the Norse sagas— have you done any reading in those old books, Hilde?—

HILDE: Oh yes, of course . . .

SOLNESS: Well, do you remember?—in all those books they always talked about the Vikings, and they described how the Vikings went to foreign countries and set fire to the countryside and robbed and stole and beat men to death—

HILDE: —and seized the women!—

SOLNESS: —took them away!—

HILDE: —carried them off on their ships—

SOLNESS: —and made love to them passionately night after night . . .

HILDE *(Stares in front of her with a half-veiled look)*: It must have been great.

SOLNESS: To seize women?—

HILDE: No—to *be seized*—

SOLNESS: Well, the reason I brought up the subject of the Vikings is that they really *had* those consciences that were strong and robust! I mean, when they got home from a day of plundering, they could just sit down cheerfully and eat a good meal! They ate, they drank—they were like happy little children after a day of playing! And you know those women whom they'd carried off—do you remember this?—in so many of those stories those women became so attached to those men that they refused to be parted from them! Does that make any sort of sense to you, Hilde?

HILDE: It makes *complete* sense to me.

SOLNESS: So—you can imagine making that sort of a choice yourself, then?

HILDE: Well, why wouldn't I?

SOLNESS: You could just make the choice to move in and live with someone who'd *violated* you?

HILDE: If I'd come to love him—yes.

SOLNESS: Oh, Hilde. Hilde. You're like a wild bird of the forest, Hilde.

HILDE: No, I'm not—because I don't fly off and hide in the shrubbery.

SOLNESS: Yes—perhaps you're more like a bird of prey.

HILDE: Yes—perhaps something more like—that sort of bird. And why shouldn't I be? Why shouldn't I go off in search of my prey, why shouldn't I seize the prize I want so desperately? If I'm able to take it in my claws and subdue it to my will—why shouldn't I do that?

SOLNESS: Hilde—do you know what I feel you really are?

HILDE: A very strange little bird, I suppose you're going to say.

SOLNESS: No. You're like—a day which is dawning, Hilde. When I look at you—it's as if I were looking—at the sun—rising . . .

(He comes close to her. She goes to Ragnar's portfolio and brings it to him.)

HILDE: Here.

SOLNESS: What are you doing?

HILDE: Take them.

SOLNESS: Why? What do you—?

HILDE: Take them.

SOLNESS: But—but—I've been looking at these drawings all day long!

HILDE: Yes, I know, but now you're going to write on them for him.

SOLNESS: Write on them? Not in a million years, Hilde!

HILDE: Not when that old man is lying in bed face to face with death? My God—can't you just offer one moment of happiness to that old man and his son before they're separated for good? I mean, even if you don't really like the drawings, surely you can bring yourself to lie a little . . .

SOLNESS: Oh, I see. Now you're asking me to lie. I see.

HILDE: And I mean, if you do write something nice on the young man's drawings, then that might actually help him to get the job of building the house.

SOLNESS: It might help him to get the job!?! Hilde, don't you understand this? That's the only reason he wants me to write on the drawings! To get the job! To get the job!

HILDE: All right, that's enough! Stop that! Stop it!

(Silence.)

SOLNESS: You want me to lie? Well, maybe for his old father's sake I could do something like that. Because at one point in the past, when I was rising up, Hilde, I pulled that old man down. I pulled him down and destroyed him.

HILDE: Really. Him, too.

SOLNESS: And now *Ragnar* would like to rise up . . .

HILDE: Yes, but if the poor fellow has no talent . . .

SOLNESS: If Ragnar rises up, I'm going to go down. Oh yes, he'll destroy me, just the way I destroyed his father.

HILDE: Destroy you? What—you mean, he actually *does* have talent?

SOLNESS *(After a moment's pause)*: Oh yes, there's no question about that. Enormous talent. Enormous talent. And I'm afraid that the forces that help people and serve them are not going to be obeying my wishes anymore.

HILDE: Then you'll have to set out on your own, Master Builder. That's all you *can* do.

SOLNESS: But, without help? That's hopeless, Hilde. This is it, you see—this is the moment it all turns around.

HILDE: No—don't say that! Are you trying to take my life away from me? Or—God!—the thing—the thing that means more to me than life itself?

SOLNESS: What is *that*?

HILDE: To see you standing with a wreath in your hand, high, high up on an enormous tower!

(Silence.)

(Once more calm) So. Write. Write really nice things for this awful Ragnar . . .

(Silence, as Solness writes several lines.)

SOLNESS *(Still writing)*: So, tell me, Hilde—have you ever— been in love?

HILDE: Say that again?

SOLNESS: I mean, in the course of your life, have you never— *loved* anyone?

(Pause.)

HILDE: Anyone else, you mean?

(Long silence.)

SOLNESS: Anyone—else . . .

(Silence.)

HILDE: Of course I've liked other men slightly, for a little while, you know, particularly when I was angry at you because you didn't come to find me—ha ha ha—I'm sure you understand . . .

(Silence. Mrs. Solness comes in, with several packages.)

MRS. SOLNESS: I've brought these *little* things back for you myself, Miss Wangel. And then all the large things will be delivered a little bit later.

HILDE: Oh, that's so nice of you!

MRS. SOLNESS: The least I could do.

SOLNESS *(Reads through what he's written)*: Aline?

MRS. SOLNESS: Yes?

SOLNESS: Did you happen to notice whether—mm—the book-keeper was out there?

MRS. SOLNESS: Of course she was out there.

SOLNESS: Ah.

MRS. SOLNESS: She was bent over her documents—her usual pose when I'm in the vicinity.

SOLNESS: Well, I'm going to give her—mm—this—and tell her that the—

HILDE *(Taking the portfolio from him)*: No—let me have the pleasure of doing that! Er—what was her name?

SOLNESS: Her name is—Miss Fosli.

HILDE: Argh, that's horribly cold. I mean her first name.

SOLNESS: It's—er—Kaya.

HILDE *(Calls toward the office)*: Kaya! Please come in right away! The Master Builder wants to speak with you.

(Kaya comes in.)

KAYA: Yes?

HILDE *(Hands Kaya the portfolio)*: Well, Kaya, you can take these now. The Master Builder has written various things on them.

KAYA: Oh—so he's finally—

SOLNESS: Bring them to Old Brovik as quickly as you can.

KAYA: Yes, I'll—

SOLNESS: Good. So Ragnar will have his chance to build something . . .

KAYA: Would it—would it be all right for him to come over, then, and—and thank you right away?

SOLNESS: No! I'm sorry. I don't want any thanks. Please send him my greetings and tell him that specifically.

KAYA: Yes—all right . . .

SOLNESS: And you can also tell him that I—I won't be needing him here from now on. And I won't be needing you either.

KAYA *(Soft, trembling)*: Won't be needing *me*? . . .

SOLNESS: Well, you're going to have a great many concerns of your own to be thinking about now. You know, thinking about and taking *care* of. So you should really go on home right now—take the drawings. The sooner the better.

(Pause. She still hasn't left.)

Don't you think you should go?

KAYA *(Still in the same state)*: Right—all right. —Mrs. Solness— *(She goes out)*

MRS. SOLNESS: God, what sneaky eyes that girl has.

SOLNESS: Oh no, no, that's quite unfair . . .

MRS. SOLNESS: Are you really letting them go, then?

SOLNESS: Oh yes, I am. But I don't want you to concern yourself with any of that, Aline, because I just want *you* to be
thinking about the fact that we're going to be moving into
our new house. And I want to make that move as soon as
possible. We are going to raise the wreath *tonight. (Turns
to Hilde)* We'll raise it up to the top of the tower! Now
what do you think about *that*, Miss Hilde?

HILDE: It will be unbelievably beautiful to see you high up in
the sky again.

SOLNESS: Me?

MRS. SOLNESS: My God in Heaven, Miss Wangel, don't even
think about something like that. My husband?—he suffers from the most terrible dizziness—he—

HILDE: Your husband suffers from dizziness? Oh no—he doesn't.

MRS. SOLNESS: But—he *does*—he *does*—

HILDE: But I saw him myself at the top of an incredibly tall
church tower!

MRS. SOLNESS: Well, I've heard people telling that story, but—
it's absolutely impossible.

SOLNESS: Yes! Impossible! Absolutely impossible! And yet—
well—I actually was up there!

MRS. SOLNESS: But how can you say that? Really, Halvard. You
can't even go out on our balcony here! One flight up!
That's the way you've always been!

SOLNESS: Well, you might perhaps have the opportunity to see
a different side of me tonight . . .

MRS. SOLNESS: No! No! God save me from that! I *won't* see
that! Because I'm going to write a note to the doctor right

this minute, and he will definitely persuade you not to do that!

SOLNESS: Aline, please—

MRS. SOLNESS: Because, you see, you really *are* sick, Halvard. The way you're talking—I mean, that's the only explanation! My God, it's so awful—dear God— *(She goes out)*

HILDE: So. Is that true?

SOLNESS: What?—that I don't like high places? that I get dizzy? Yes. *(She is facing forward, looking out)* What are you looking at?

HILDE *(Pointing out)*: I'm looking at that very small room at the top of the tower.

SOLNESS: Yes, that could be *your* room, couldn't it, Hilde? You could live up there like a little princess.

HILDE: Well, that's what you promised me.

SOLNESS: Yes? Did I?

(Hilde leaves. The lights begin to change. Solness speaks to the audience. As he speaks, Mrs. Solness comes in and takes a seat facing out toward the audience.)

And then a few hours pass, and it's late in the afternoon, and Aline sits by herself on the second-floor veranda, looking out at the garden and the new house.

(She sits for a while, and then Hilde comes in holding flowers. She seems to be about to speak to Mrs. Solness but turns to the audience instead.)

HILDE: Let's take another fifteen minutes.

(Intermission.)

PART THREE

Mrs. Solness sits looking out toward the audience, as before. Hilde comes in with flowers and approaches Mrs. Solness.

MRS. SOLNESS: So—have you been taking a walk in the garden, Miss Wangel?

HILDE: Mmm—looking around a bit . . .

MRS. SOLNESS: I see you found some flowers . . .

HILDE: Yes, definitely! There are lots of them down there. You know, growing up between the bushes . . .

MRS. SOLNESS: Really? They're still growing? Well well. You see, I almost never go down there . . .

HILDE: No? You don't? I mean—don't you at least run down there—once each day?

MRS. SOLNESS: Well I must say, running isn't something I really do now.

HILDE: But I mean—don't you at least go down there once in a while?—just to say hello to all the lovely things?

69

MRS. SOLNESS: Well, it's all become alien territory, as far as I'm concerned. I'd feel almost—uncomfortable—about seeing it again.

HILDE: Your own garden?

MRS. SOLNESS: Oh, I don't think of it as mine at all, you see, now.

HILDE: You mean you don't—

MRS. SOLNESS: Oh no, it's certainly not mine. Oh no, no— It's not the way it was in my mother and father's time. Not at all. They've gotten rid of so much of the garden, Miss Wangel, it's pitiable, really. —I mean, imagine what they've done—they've parceled it all out, you see, and built houses for strangers, houses for people I don't even know—and then these strangers, you see, can sit at their windows and just *stare* at me. Isn't that something?

(Pause.)

HILDE: Mrs. Solness?

MRS. SOLNESS: Yes?

HILDE: Would it be all right with you if I sat with you here for a short while?

MRS. SOLNESS: Yes, that would be very nice—if you feel you would like to.

(Hilde sits down near Mrs. Solness.)

HILDE *(Sighs)*: What a perfect spot to just sit and sun yourself—like a cat . . .

MRS. SOLNESS: It's so kind of you—to want to sit with me. I would have thought you'd be going in now to be with my husband . . .

HILDE: What would you think I'd be doing with him?

MRS. SOLNESS: Oh, I thought you'd be—helping him, I suppose.

HILDE: Oh, please! No! Anyway, he isn't in there. He's gone over to see the men who are working on the new house.

And the expression he had on his face!—he looked so fierce and dangerous—I really didn't have the courage to speak to him.

MRS. SOLNESS: Oh! Ha ha—is that right? But do you know?—he really has the most gentle disposition in the whole world.

HILDE: He does?!

MRS. SOLNESS: You see, you don't really know him properly yet, Miss Wangel.

(Silence.)

HILDE: So—Are you happy to be moving over into the new house?

MRS. SOLNESS: Oh, I ought to be. Because he *so* much wants me to be happy about it . . .

HILDE: But—I'm sure that's not the only reason to *be* happy— is it?

MRS. SOLNESS: Oh yes. Yes it is. Because you see, that's my simple obligation in life, Miss Wangel—to do—what he wants. Simply—to yield . . . But there are many occasions when it's terribly hard to beat one's spirit into the necessary submission.

HILDE: Ergh—yes—that *must* be hard . . .

MRS. SOLNESS: That's one thing you can certainly be sure about—it is hard. I mean, if one isn't a better person than I am, at any rate.

(Pause.)

HILDE: Mrs. Solness—when someone has been through really hard times the way you have—

MRS. SOLNESS: How do you know I've been through hard times?

HILDE: Your husband said you had . . .

MRS. SOLNESS: Hm . . . to me he says so little about those things. But yes, it's true, I've been through quite a bit in the course of my life, Miss Wangel—yes, I have.

HILDE: Dear Mrs. Solness— First everything burned up in the fire? . . .

MRS. SOLNESS (*With a sigh*): Yes. Everything I had.

HILDE: And then—what was—so much worse—the—

MRS. SOLNESS (*Looks questioningly at her*): Worse?

HILDE: What happened—which was worse than—

MRS. SOLNESS: What do you mean?

HILDE (*Softly*): I meant—losing the boys . . .

MRS. SOLNESS: Oh—that—yes . . . Yes, well, that is really something different, you see. That was really a sort of—decision by a higher power. And one has to submit oneself to something like that. And even give thanks for it.

HILDE: Do you—do that?

MRS. SOLNESS: Mmm—not always—unfortunately. I know it's my obligation, that's what I ought to do. And yet, sometimes, I just can't.

HILDE: But I think that's so understandable—really.

MRS. SOLNESS: And again and again I have to say to myself, It was a just punishment.

HILDE: But—why? . . .

MRS. SOLNESS: Because when I was face to face with what was difficult, I wasn't strong.

HILDE: I don't understand . . .

MRS. SOLNESS: Quite honestly, Miss Wangel—please don't keep talking about the two little boys—we really should only be happy for them, because things are so good for them now—very very good. (*Pause*) And of course it's the *little* losses which really break your heart in life—when you lose certain things which other people might consider almost—worthless, but which for you . . .

HILDE: Dear sweet Mrs. Solness—tell me. Please.

MRS. SOLNESS: Oh—as I said—just unimportant things. You know. All the old portraits that were on the walls—they were all burnt up. And all the old silk dresses—they were burned—you know, all the dresses which had belonged to the family for such a long long time. And all the lacework which had been done by all the mothers and the grand-mothers—all of it burnt. And you can imagine—the jewelry, of course. *(Heavily)* And then—all the dolls.

HILDE: The dolls?

MRS. SOLNESS: I had nine beautiful dolls.

HILDE: And they burned, too?

MRS. SOLNESS: Yes—every one of them. And that was pain-ful—that was very painful for me.

HILDE: So you'd always kept the dolls you had as a young girl?

MRS. SOLNESS: I didn't just—keep them. I would take them out—and look at them—hold them—play with them—

HILDE: Even after you were grown up?

MRS. SOLNESS: Yes—long after.

HILDE: Even after you were married?

MRS. SOLNESS: Yes. Only when he couldn't see me, of course. But then—they were burnt. The poor little things were burnt. Nobody made any attempt to save *them*. Oh God, it's so awful to imagine them burning . . . Don't laugh at me.

HILDE: No—

MRS. SOLNESS: Because in a way—they were—alive . . . I carried them around—in my arms—like small children—not quite born yet . . .

(Dr. Herdal comes in.)

DR. HERDAL: Well—ah—so, Mrs. Solness—so you're sitting outside and letting yourself catch a cold—is that it?

MRS. SOLNESS: Oh no—it's nice and warm out here today.

DR. HERDAL: Hm, I suppose. But you sent me a note? Is there some sort of problem, or—?

MRS. SOLNESS *(Stands up)*: Yes, I have to talk to you about something.

DR. HERDAL: All right . . . *(To Hilde)* Ha ha—I see you've put on your mountain climbing uniform today—ha ha ha—

HILDE *(Merrily, standing up also)*: Absolutely! And every button is polished! Ha ha ha—of course *I* won't be climbing—I won't be breaking *my* neck today. I mean, you and I are just going to stay down here on level ground and watch, aren't we, Doctor?

DR. HERDAL: And what are we going to be watching, I wonder?

MRS. SOLNESS: For God's sake, will you stop talking about that? *(To Hilde)* Please—please just try to get that idea out of his head. *(Pause)* I think that we ought to be—friends, Miss Wangel. Don't you think that we *can* be?

HILDE *(Throwing her arms passionately around Mrs. Solness)*: Oh—if we could be—that would be so wonderful!

MRS. SOLNESS *(Gently freeing herself)*: Yes—yes.

(She leads Dr. Herdal off. Solness appears.)

SOLNESS: Have you ever noticed that the minute I show up somewhere, my wife leaves?

HILDE: Actually, I've noticed that the minute you show up somewhere, you drive her out.

SOLNESS: Oh, maybe. But that's completely out of my control, I'm afraid.

HILDE: Tell me—why did you come up here just now?

SOLNESS: To see you.

HILDE: But surely you saw that I was here with *her* . . .

SOLNESS: Well—I knew she'd leave.

HILDE *(After a pause)*: But—doesn't it upset you that she would run away from you like that?

SOLNESS: Sometimes it makes life easier.

HILDE: It's easier when she isn't there—

SOLNESS: Mmm . . .

HILDE: —so you don't have to see—her suffering.

SOLNESS: Right.

(Hilde looks out toward the front.)

(After a pause) Did you talk with her for a long time?

(She stands unmoving and doesn't answer.)

Was it a long—conversation?

(She is silent.)

Hilde?—what did she talk about?

(She is silent.)

Poor Aline! I'm sure she mentioned the boys—obviously.

(A nervous shudder runs through Hilde.)

Never get over it! She'll never get over it! She'll never get over it! *(He approaches Hilde)* You're standing there like a statue—just the way you looked last evening when—

HILDE: I want to leave.

SOLNESS: Leave!

HILDE: Yes.

SOLNESS: But you can't! I—

HILDE: But what am I going to do here?

SOLNESS: Hilde! Just *be* here!

HILDE: Oh, for God's sake. You *know* it wouldn't stay like that!

SOLNESS: Well—?

HILDE: No! I can't do something that wrong against someone I know! I—to take something—that belongs to her—I can't do it!

SOLNESS: But why do you—

HILDE *(Continuing)*: If she were a stranger, someone I'd never met, it might be different, but someone I've come close to— No! I can't! I'm sorry—I'm leaving.

SOLNESS: But what will become of *me*, then? What will I have to live for? After you leave?

HILDE: But you don't have to worry about that. You *have* something. —You have the debt you have to pay—your obligation—to her. Live for that.

SOLNESS: No—it's too late. Because Aline is dead. Because of me, she's dead. The last drops of blood have been drained out of her body, and now I'm living my life chained to someone who is actually dead! —But I'm still capable of experiencing joy! Help me! Help me! I'm still alive!

(A long silence.)

HILDE: So—what are you planning to build after this?

SOLNESS: Build? Oh, there probably won't *be* that much more after this . . .

HILDE: So you're not planning to build more nice, cozy homes for nice mothers and fathers and children?

SOLNESS: In a way I wonder whether people in the future will have any desire for something like that. Because a home is not what people need. A home doesn't bring happiness or joy to people. I wouldn't have been happy if I'd somehow managed to have a home.

HILDE: Poor Master Builder. What a conclusion to come to— when you've devoted all these years to building those homes—and poured your life into it—

SOLNESS: Yes—

(A pause.)

HILDE *(Suddenly bursting out)*: Oh Christ, I just think—

SOLNESS: What?

HILDE: —I think it's ridiculous not to have the courage to reach out and take happiness, just *take* it, and *life*, life *itself*—just because there's someone in the way whom you happen to know . . .

SOLNESS: . . . someone whom you don't have the right to leave . . .

HILDE: Or is it possible that that's *not* true?—that the truth is, you really always *do* have that right? But then, that would—it— Oh God, if only one could just fall asleep, and the whole thing could—the whole thing could . . .

(She closes her eyes. They both are silent for a long time. Then:)

(Drowsily) Hm. I know what you're going to build next, Master Builder.

SOLNESS: Really? What?

HILDE: It's going to be a palace.

(A long silence.)

SOLNESS: Tell me how you imagine it, Hilde . . .

HILDE *(Slowly)*: My palace will stand very, very high, up on a hill. Nothing around it on any side, so I can see far, far off—way out over the land—

SOLNESS: And I'm sure there will be a high tower on it?

HILDE: Yes. Oh yes. The tower, you see, will be frightfully high. And way, way up on the top of the tower—yes, a balcony will be there, encircling the whole thing. And outside on that balcony I'm going to stand—

SOLNESS: Oh my God! That you would *stand* up there—so horribly high up—so dizzyingly high up—

HILDE: Yes! That's where I'll stand—and of course you'll be able to come up also . . .

SOLNESS: The Master Builder will be allowed—to come up to the princess?

HILDE: Yes, of course . . .

SOLNESS: But he won't be able to build anymore!—poor Master Builder . . .

HILDE: Oh no—he *will* build—because you see, Master Builder, you and I are going to be partners now! And we're going to build these very special structures that will be more beautiful, really, than anything on earth—

SOLNESS: Really? You mean—

HILDE: Oh yes, Master Builder, we're going to be building dream palaces that will be able to stand firmly right in the middle of the sky . . . They'll stand firmly in the middle of the sky . . .

(Ragnar comes out, carrying a large wreath with flowers and silk ribbons wound around it.)

Oh, look! Look! Oh, it's going to be so incredibly beautiful! . . .

SOLNESS: But—how do *you* come to be bringing the wreath, Ragnar?

RAGNAR: Well, I promised the foreman I would.

SOLNESS: So—is your father doing a bit better, then?

RAGNAR: Mmm—not really.

SOLNESS: But—did the things I wrote cheer him up at all?

RAGNAR: No, they came too late, I'm sorry to say.

SOLNESS: Oh!—you mean—

RAGNAR: When Kaya arrived, he was already in a coma. He'd had a stroke, actually.

SOLNESS: But for God's sake—go home and take care of him! I—

RAGNAR: Well, there's nothing more I can do for him now.

SOLNESS: But you ought to be *with* him—you ought—

RAGNAR: Well, *she's* with him—she's sitting by the bed and—

SOLNESS: You mean, Kaya?

RAGNAR *(Looks darkly at Solness)*: Yes—Kaya.

SOLNESS: If you don't mind, I'll take this down to the men. *(He takes the wreath)* And, you know, I actually don't have anything for you to do here today.

RAGNAR: Yes, I know that, but I'm going to stay for the ceremony.

SOLNESS: Oh. Well, all right then.

(He leaves with the wreath. Hilde stares after him for a moment, then turns to Ragnar.)

HILDE: I would have thought you might have thanked him, at least.

RAGNAR: Thanked him? You think I should have thanked him?

HILDE: Yes—of course . . .

RAGNAR: You're probably the one I should actually thank—am I right?

HILDE: What do you mean?

RAGNAR (*Without answering her*): But—can I say?—I think you ought to proceed with caution . . . Because I'd be very surprised if you really know him yet.

HILDE: I know him better than anyone in the world knows him.

RAGNAR: Incredible—ha ha—thank him . . . Can I tell you something? This is the man who has kept me down at the lowest level, year after year—he made my father lose his respect for me—he made me lose whatever respect I once might have had for myself! And do you know what the point of it all was?

HILDE: Please tell me.

RAGNAR: The point of it all was to keep her here with him!

HILDE: What? Your fiancée? Kaya?

RAGNAR: She told me herself today!

HILDE: No! That's not true! That's a lie!

RAGNAR: Yes. She told me that he literally controls her soul— she can never let him go—she has to be with him—

HILDE: No! No! That won't be permitted. And you've misunderstood the whole situation. He was keeping *her* here simply to keep hold of *you*. He needed to keep you there in the office. You—not her. Now that is the truth—that is the truth— and I'm not going to stand for any other explanation!

RAGNAR: But then—could it actually be possible that for all this time he was somehow afraid of what I would be able to do? He knew I would be a good architect! Oh my God— what a pitiful man. He's a pitiful, weak, cowardly man.

HILDE: You—

RAGNAR: He's afraid of *me*, an unknown young architect whom he trained himself—he's afraid of climbing up that tower over there on his own house—

HILDE: No! No! He's *not* afraid. Because I once saw him climb up an *enormous* tower and tie a wreath to a church's weather vane . . .

RAGNAR: What? You saw him do that?

HILDE: *And* he's going to do it again—tonight! We're all going to see it . . .

RAGNAR: Well, that is something we'll never see . . .

HILDE: But it's what I want to see! I have to see him do that!

RAGNAR: Yes, but unfortunately, he won't. He can't. Maybe he could at one time, but now, he can't.

(Mrs. Solness comes in.)

MRS. SOLNESS: Where is he? I—

RAGNAR: He's with the men who are working down there.

HILDE: He took the wreath, and—

MRS. SOLNESS: He took the wreath? Oh my God, Brovik, you have to go down there. Tell him he needs to come back here right away . . .

RAGNAR: Should I say that you need to speak with him, or—?

MRS. SOLNESS: Just tell him to come up here . . .

RAGNAR: All right, Mrs. Solness. *(He goes off)*

MRS. SOLNESS: I don't think you can even imagine the anxiety I feel because of him—what I have to live with—I—

HILDE: But—is this really something—so absolutely terrifying? —I mean—

MRS. SOLNESS: Of course it's terrifying! What if he actually has gotten it into his head that he's going to go up that scaffolding?

(Dr. Herdal comes in.)

DR. HERDAL: I'm afraid you're going to have to come in now.

MRS. SOLNESS: No, I can't.

DR. HERDAL: But some women have just arrived—they've come to see you.

MRS. SOLNESS: Oh my God, they've come *now?* Oh no—

DR. HERDAL: They've come to watch the ceremony, it seems . . .

MRS. SOLNESS: Yes, yes—I mean, it's my obligation to look after them, obviously—I have to go in there—I—

HILDE: But—can't you just ask them to leave?

MRS. SOLNESS: Oh no, no, that's impossible. I mean, they've come to my house, it's certainly my obligation to look after them—of course— *(To Hilde)* But—but you stay out here—and when he comes up here, just don't let him go—hold on to him!

HILDE: But wouldn't it be more appropriate for you to do that?

MRS. SOLNESS: Of course! Yes! My God, of course I should do it, it's my obligation to take care of him, *my* obligation, I *know* that, but—but—there are so many things I'm supposed to be doing—I—it's unbelievable that I have to go to see these women now!

(Mrs. Solness and Dr. Herdal go off. Hilde stands for a while, looking out front. Solness comes in.)

SOLNESS: It's all looking marvelous down there. Mr. Tesman, the foreman, is going to go up the tower with the wreath. I heard Aline was looking for me—?

HILDE: No—I don't think so.

SOLNESS: Because Ragnar said—

HILDE *(Interrupting)*: So—is it true?

SOLNESS: What?

HILDE: The bookkeeper? Kaya?

(He doesn't answer.)

(Violently) You pathetic creature!

SOLNESS *(Stunned)*: Hilde—I can't live if you see me that way!

HILDE: Well, then let me see you differently! Let me see you up there on that tower—high up and standing free!

SOLNESS: Hilde, no!—I can't!—

HILDE: Well, that is what I want! That is what I want! . . . And you did it once. You did it. I saw you.

SOLNESS: Hilde, don't you understand? I was in such a state then because of what had been done to me, the death of my children, that I did something—something that was *impossible*. It was impossible for me, but I did it—I—

HILDE: Yes?

SOLNESS: Hilde, I don't even know how I got up there. But when I was up there at the top, I made a vow—I vowed that I would never build churches again—only homes, where *people* could live . . . And then I came down, and that was when your father had us all to tea, and I met you.

HILDE: Yes. Yes.

SOLNESS: Oh Hilde, my God, if I were to try it?—if I were to try to climb that tower tonight? Do you know what I'd vow tonight at the top of the tower? I'd vow that I'd never build *homes* again, but instead I'd devote myself to building the only structures that can actually contain human happiness—

HILDE: Yes, that's right—

SOLNESS: —those extraordinary, beautiful palaces that stand firmly in the middle of the sky . . . And I would vow to build them—together with a princess—whom I love . . . And then, after I made that vow, I'd wave wildly to everyone below, and I'd come down, and I'd throw my arms around my princess's neck, and I'd kiss her and kiss her again and again . . .

HILDE: My Master Builder . . . My Master Builder . . .

(Now we can hear again the weird music we heard earlier when Solness fell into his dream. Mrs. Solness comes out, dressed for the ceremony, along with Dr. Herdal and the actresses who earlier played Nurse Olga, Nurse Nora, Nurse Myrtle and Nurse Ingrid. They now play women from the town, and they all wear party outfits. Then Ragnar comes in.)

MRS. SOLNESS (*To Ragnar*): Are we going to have music, too?

RAGNAR: Yes—it's the band from the construction workers' association.

FIRST WOMAN: They're absolutely marvelous.

SECOND WOMAN: We haven't had such a good band in this town for years.

THIRD WOMAN: They play such great music.

FOURTH WOMAN: Yes, they practice every week.

MRS. SOLNESS: It's wonderful, isn't it?

SOLNESS (*To Ragnar*): So, is Mr. Tesman ready to climb up the tower with the wreath?

RAGNAR: Yes, he's delighted to have the honor of doing it. You know Tesman—he always finds it exciting to climb up to high places.

SOLNESS: Good. Good. I'll go down there myself now.

MRS. SOLNESS (*Anxiously*): What are you going to do down there, Halvard?

SOLNESS: Well, I need to be with the men who are working down there. I mean, that's where I usually am, on these occasions . . .

MRS. SOLNESS (*To Solness*): Be sure to tell Mr. Tesman to be very careful when he climbs up the tower. Promise me you won't forget to say that, Halvard!

(*Solness kisses her and leaves.*)

DR. HERDAL (*To Mrs. Solness*): So, you see?—I was right! He's forgotten all about that whole crazy idea of going up himself.

(*Mrs. Solness and Dr. Herdal go over to stand by the visiting women, who now stand looking out toward the audience. Hilde stands apart, also looking out. The music gets even stranger. Ragnar approaches Hilde and speaks to her quietly.*)

RAGNAR: So . . . do you see that little group of young people over there by the new house? Those are all my friends. They've come to watch Master Builder Solness *not* have the courage to climb up the tower—ha ha ha . . .

HILDE: Then they'll be disappointed.

DR. HERDAL *(Pointing)*: Look! Mr. Tesman's beginning to climb . . .

MRS. SOLNESS: Oh, and he has to carry the wreath too! It's awful—awful—he has to be *so careful*—

RAGNAR: No—it's him! It's him! Oh my God!

(They all speak rather quietly, as people do at the bedside of someone who's ill or asleep.)

MRS. SOLNESS: Halvard! No!

(As the music continues quietly, Solness comes in in his bathrobe. As Dr. Herdal, Mrs. Solness, Ragnar and Hilde look out front toward the new house, Solness, using the footstool, climbs with difficulty onto the bed. The actress who played Ingrid goes out. The other three visiting women become nurses again. They re-connect Solness to the tubes and wires to which he was originally attached. Solness breathes with difficulty. We can see that he is struggling. The nurses check the monitors and watch over him. The others don't see him.)

HILDE: Climbing higher—higher—

(Dr. Herdal goes to Solness. Mrs. Solness, Ragnar and Hilde continue to face forward, looking out.)

MRS. SOLNESS: No—no—

(Mrs. Solness goes to Solness. She sits by the bed and holds his hand.)

RAGNAR: He's *bound* to turn around—he *can't* keep going—

HILDE: Climbing—climbing—almost there . . .

(Old Brovik comes in and stands by the bed.)

There—there—the very top! . . .

(Hilde continues to face forward. Kaya comes in and stands by the bed, not too near anyone else.)

Now, hanging the wreath—speaking—now he's waving— *(Hilde waves a handkerchief and shouts)* Yes!

(Solness, in the bed, gasps. Hilde and Ragnar see Solness fall off the tower. Ragnar speaks to Hilde.)

RAGNAR: Damn—he actually was *not* able to do it, after all. He must have fallen right into the stone quarry . . .

(He goes to stand by the bed, near Old Brovik. The nurses and Dr. Herdal stop doing anything and just cluster around Solness. Nurse Ingrid comes in, in her nurse's uniform, holding a blue bottle with a red label. She rushes to Dr. Herdal.)

NURSE INGRID *(To Dr. Herdal)*: I found the bottle in the other room. It— *(She sees everyone clustered around Solness, who breathes with difficulty)* Oh—sorry.

HILDE *(Still facing forward)*: But he made it—all the way to the very top . . . My Master Builder . . .

(She goes to the bed and kisses Solness on the forehead. When she kisses him, the music abruptly stops, Solness's dream ends, and Solness stops breathing. Hilde puts on her nurse's uniform. The lighting becomes the lighting we saw at the beginning of the play. Everyone stays gathered around the bed for a while. They leave one by one until only Mrs. Solness is left with Solness. The lights slowly go out.)

END

AFTERWORD

To take a normal, contemporary bourgeois situation, imagine I am in a shop waiting at the front of a line at a cash register to buy, let's say, a book, and a man steps in front of me, apparently planning to approach the cashier before I do. The man's action provokes an emotional response in me—but, to complicate things, let's say that I don't know whether the man is intentionally breaking into the line in front of me because he doesn't respect the rules, or whether perhaps he hasn't noticed the line, has recently arrived from a different sort of society in which things are done differently, or has interpreted the situation in some other way that's unknown to me. I would like to stop the man, and I also have a variety of reactions to what's happening that I feel the need to somehow express, so I search for the appropriate words to say. I might say, "Hey! Don't do that!" I might say, "Sir, I'm not sure you realize that we're standing in a line." I might say, "Pardon me, I was here first." The possibilities are limitless, but in searching for the appropriate words, obviously I'm also searching for an appropriate identity for myself. Which words are appropriate to the person I am, or appropriate to the person I think I am, or appropriate to the person I want to become right now, or to the person I wish I were, or to the person I enjoy pretending I am?

The position of the translator bears quite a bit of similarity to the position of a person searching for appropriate words in the course of his own life. If the translator is translating a line of dialogue from a play, he is choosing appropriate words for a particular character in a particular situation, and so obviously he needs to have some sort of interpretation of the character and of the situation as well as of the words used in the original language by the original author. The original author, of course, has placed his character's line of dialogue within the framework of a particular tone—sarcastic, for example, sincere, insincere, snide, unaffected, or something more mysterious and unique—and the translator may want to imitate that, but still, a knowledge of life is needed in order to comprehend what tone the original author might possibly have been getting at. A bilingual nine year old might know many English synonyms for every Norwegian word ever used by Henrik Ibsen, and he might even have a good knowledge of Norwegian grammar and English grammar, but I doubt if he would do a very good translation of *Master Builder Solness*, for example, because his insight into the characters and situations portrayed by Ibsen would probably not be adequate.

To acknowledge that a good translator must draw on his knowledge of life, and not just of the dictionary, when he approaches each new sentence, however, seems to open up some disturbing areas of freedom for the translator.

The history of this particular translation and adaptation goes like this. I've been writing plays since 1967, and since around 1977 I've also worked as an actor. In the year 1971, the director André Gregory became the first person working in the professional theater to say that he liked my plays, and he hired me to do a fascinating job. He wanted me to adapt a play by Henrik Ibsen, *Peer Gynt*. This was thrilling to me, partly because I'd always adored Ibsen. André's company of actors had been working on *Peer Gynt* for a very long time, but the complete text of the play (originally presented by Ibsen as a book to be read rather than a script to be performed) was a vast epic, and it seemed that it could perhaps be cut. I watched the company's rehearsals for six months, and it was a joyful experience, but I couldn't figure out any way to cut or otherwise change Ibsen's text. I suggested writing a play of my own for the company instead, and I wrote a play for them called *Our Late Night*, which was the first play of mine to be publicly performed, opening at The Public Theater in New York in January of 1975.

A dozen or so years later, I found myself playing the part of Vanya in André's version of Chekhov's *Uncle Vanya*. (The translation was by David Mamet.) We rehearsed the play over the course of three or four years, without ever doing it for a paying audience, and finally Louis Malle made a film of our work called *Vanya on 42nd Street*. About a year or so after the film was released, I said to André, "Why don't you do a play by the playwright *I* like, Ibsen?" He said, "Yes, that's a good idea, but I want to pick the play." And he chose *Master Builder Solness*.

Because of the circumstances in which I was brought up, I've always been a somewhat arrogant person. From an early age, I went to schools that avoided at all costs any form of instruction that might damage the "self-esteem" of the students. So yes, I was aware that *Master Builder Solness* was written in Norwegian, but, as I knew a bit of German and had even spent enough time in Norway to know how Norwegian was pronounced, I felt I was pretty well qualified to translate the play, and I even knew exactly how I wanted to go about it. So, I went to the Norwegian consulate in New York and got hold of a Norwegian text of the play. And then I made a large photocopy of the text on very large sheets of paper. André's friend Elinor Fuchs found us a wonderful scholar of Scandinavian literature who taught in Rochester. Her name

was Sandra Saari, and at my request she wrote English synonyms for all the words in the text—a few synonyms for each
word, if possible—in very small handwriting next to the Norwegian words on the very large sheets of paper. Sandra, André
and I then talked through the text, with Sandra explaining
all sorts of interesting things—for example, that a given Norwegian word, unlike its English synonym, was always used to
mean X and never to mean Y, or that a certain word was an
archaic word used in Norse mythology and was not an every-
day modern word, or that a certain word was used by most
people to mean A but was often used by Ibsen to mean B.
I then proceeded to turn the large sheets of paper into an English text. This took me a couple of years. Finally, I met with
a kindly academic expert who checked my translation line
by line, so that at least I knew that I'd understood the literal
meaning of each of Ibsen's lines, even if I'd translated some
of them in an idiosyncratic way.

The purpose of the translation was to provide a text that
a group of actors under André Gregory's direction could perform. In other words, I was trying to write something that
would be the basis for a wonderful production that people
today or in the future would see, while at the same time
I attempted to give an honest account of Ibsen's play, written
in the past. When I presented André with my text in 1997,
each line expressed more or less what Ibsen's equivalent line
had expressed, though, in the writing of each line, my hope
was always to use words that could be believably spoken by
people today (without ever using the sort of slang that would
permanently affix the line to a particular time and place) and
also to write words that when spoken by a character would
strike someone today as psychologically plausible.

A translation of the play Ibsen completed in 1892 into
dialogue that would sound to a contemporary audience like
believable contemporary speech would have to be to a certain
extent false to the feeling and atmosphere of the original text.
Contemporary speech carries with it associations unknown to

Ibsen and assumptions unknown to Ibsen, and it inevitably uses words that had no exact equivalents in Ibsen's time.

Now, one very exciting fact about writing for the theater is that a playwright can hope that his plays, because they will be reinterpreted by actors, directors, and even translators, can retain for audiences living in different times and places the full power that may be locked within them. A playwright can hope that even after he's dead, an audience may watch his play in some country he never visited, in a language he never knew, and if it's done well enough, they'll be so involved in the characters and the story that they'll forget that the play was originally written in a different time and place. The price the playwright pays for this wonderful hope is that the play that the audience will see, if he's lucky enough to have this rare and remarkable post-death experience, will be to one degree or another not exactly what he originally imagined. And yet this is true to some extent of all productions of a play, and it's a source of pleasure for the playwright more often than uneasiness, because it's usually a great delight for a writer to see his words interpreted in an unexpected way by other artists, and indeed the wise playwright has written words that are not complete in themselves but call for an actor's contribution.

My own situation as translator of *Master Builder Solness* was perhaps a somewhat special case, because of my particular arrogance, and because of my particular ignorance. My ignorance of the Norwegian language and my ignorance about Norwegian literature, combined with my ignorance about life and behavior in Norway in 1892, meant that I couldn't possibly capture the exact nuance and mood of each of Ibsen's lines. I was like a painter who had set up his easel on a high hill overlooking a valley where an intriguing group of people were having a picnic, but it was as if I, as the painter, instead of painting the valley as a whole, with a few people indistinctly seen at the bottom of the frame, had decided to do a large, detailed portrait simply of the picnic, showing in detail the particular expressions on the faces of the people, the drops of wine on the necks of the bottles, and the crumbs of bread spilling on to the grass—details that inevitably had to be made up. In other words, from the moment I took on the task of translating *Master Builder Solness*, it was inevitable that I'd be involving myself in some sort of collaboration with Henrik Ibsen. And consciously or unconsciously, I guess this was really what I had wanted all along.

This statement is neither a defiant boast that mocks the potential concerns of sincere Ibsen scholars, nor is it the abject confession of a repentant criminal who knows that what he's done was wrong. I don't yet know how bad I should feel about what I've done. I know that Stravinsky's *Pulcinella Suite* has always been one of my favorite pieces of music. It's an instrumental work that Stravinsky took from a ballet he'd written in which he reinterpreted and recombined music that had been written by one or more eighteenth-century Italian composers (when Stravinsky wrote his ballet, all the music was thought to have been written by Pergolesi, though scholars today don't think it was). And what I did was much less extreme than what Stravinsky did. You could almost—almost—say that it had more in common with something like re-scoring one of Bach's organ works for full orchestra, as Arnold Schoenberg did, or playing harpsichord music on a piano. It wasn't as extreme as what Stravinsky did, but all the same, I know I wouldn't want anyone to do it to me. If I heard that another writer was "collaborating" on one of my plays, I'd be extremely upset. And yet, without implicitly accepting the fact that there would be a collaboration between me and Ibsen, André and I couldn't and wouldn't have embarked on the project of doing Ibsen's play, a project that ultimately took fifteen years and resulted not in a theatrical presentation of the play (at least not so far) but in a film.

At any rate, once the idea of "collaboration" between Ibsen and me was accepted, it was probably inevitable that the role of the living collaborator would grow, while the role of the dead collaborator would not.

I had originally imagined that I would simply deliver my translation to André and that I would not be involved in the project beyond that, but, partly because I found I had an overwhelming desire to do it, André decided that I ought to play the part of Solness, and so that's what happened. We started work on the play in 1997. The younger members of the cast changed between 1997 and 2012, when we made the film, but Julie Hagerty (Mrs. Solness), Larry Pine (Dr. Herdal), and I worked on the play with André during all those years. Each of us did many other things in each of those years, and there were years that had more Ibsen in them than others, but we never stopped seizing three weeks here and a month there to devote to *Master Builder Solness*, and even when we were not together, we kept working on the play in the workshops of our unconscious minds, which is an essential part of André's method. (It does work, the proof being that when we would meet after a long interval we would find that we could easily do certain sections of the play that had seemed horribly difficult or impossible when we'd last been together.) From very early on, we all thought that what we were doing might work very well as a film. So much of the play was made up of scenes involving intimately shared thoughts, scenes that seemed to cry out for close-ups.

As the years passed, I became aware that I had spent quite a large section of my life on this play. And that awareness couldn't help adding to my feeling that I knew the play awfully well and perhaps had the right to make some changes in the text.

Now, it's an interesting fact about Ibsen that he wrote in a marvelously economical style, using as few words as possible to say what he had to say, and yet he loved to repeat what he had said, using repetition almost the way composers of music do. I had realized early on that I couldn't imitate Ibsen's economy of words, because when I tried to use only the small number of words that Ibsen used, the characters sounded crude and at times not very bright, and Ibsen himself even seemed a bit wooden or lacking in grace. In writing his original line, Ibsen could select a small number of Norwegian words that would perfectly combine the tone he wanted with the meaning he wanted. If I was clever enough to be able to find a small number of English words that would match the original meaning, they certainly wouldn't also capture the right tone. I'm not claiming that no writer in English could possibly have used the same number of words that Ibsen used while still displaying the full intelligence and emotional range of Ibsen and his characters—I'm just saying that I was dubious about whether such a great master of writing lived among us, and I'm saying that I knew I was not that master. So I used more words than Ibsen used, and this meant that my text would have taken four hours or so to perform. That fact in itself meant that it was probably always a likelihood that one day I'd begin to make some cuts in the text. As for the strange, circular, somewhat vertigo-inducing repetitions characteristic of Ibsen, they were of course fascinating and in a way mesmerizing, but also, to us, as we rehearsed the play, they were in a certain way maddening or even unbearable. The way in which he would approach a fact or a story through a hint, then through another hint from a different angle, and then another hint again, must have had a certain extraordinary suspense-inducing power when his plays were originally performed, but for us, particularly in my excessively long translation, the repetitions often seemed to represent an obsessive habit that begged to be restrained.

The issue of the ending of the play had also always loomed as a problem for us. Oddly, the more we rehearsed, the quieter and less "theatrical" our way of doing the play became. In any case, the type of theater André and I liked to do was on a very small scale. (For example, we had done my play *The Designated Mourner* for an audience of forty people a night.) In Ibsen's time, plays were done on large stages of a kind we would never have wanted to use (and I must say, would never have been invited to use). But the crucial stage direction at the very end of the play calls for a body to fall from a great height through a large group of trees. We always knew that this stage direction represented a puzzle to which we would have to find a solution.

And let's be brutally frank. There were certain things in the original text that did not grow on me over the years. I never could accept that when Solness argued out loud with God on top of the church tower in Hilde's hometown, his voice could sound like the playing of harps. And there were passages that for me remained not alive—dead zones through which I impatiently had to pass before returning to the story that had so deeply fascinated me. If I myself felt uninterested in these passages after we'd tried for years to do our best for them, should we really just mindlessly go ahead and present them to an audience?

Of course I'm aware of the fact that throughout the centuries gangsters and petty criminals, corrupt officials and collaborators with evil regimes, have explained their actions to themselves by saying, I know it isn't good to do what I'm doing, but I'm not doing it because I *enjoy* doing it, I'm doing it for the sake of people I care about—my children, my elderly parents, my fellow citizens, etc. So, when I heard myself thinking to myself, I'm going to change this passage for the sake of the audience, I knew that I was doing something that might possibly be wrong, and yet it really is a terrible thing to ask people to come into a room where a play will be done, and then to make that whole room full of people sit through minutes in which they receive little or nothing of value to them, minutes that are giving little or nothing to actually anyone in the room, neither the people watching the play, nor the people performing the play. In our case, who would it be serving, really, if those lifeless minutes distanced the audience from the play, forced them to become less interested in the play, less involved in the play, less enchanted by Ibsen's story, less admiring of Ibsen himself? If Ibsen had come back to life and joined us in our rehearsal room, would he not have wanted something to be done about the moments in the play that were falling flat?

So I made small changes in the play, and then eventually I made a very substantial change in the play by putting Solness on his deathbed from the very beginning and explicitly defining everything that happens after Hilde's knock on the door as a dream Solness dreams before he dies. André had always felt that the play was about a man's confrontation with himself as he approaches death. This made that explicit.

Master Builder Solness is a dream, whether you call it a dream or you don't call it a dream, and it seemed better to call it a dream. (Of course, my hope is that people watching this version of *Master Builder Solness* will know that the story of Hilde is a dream, but that they'll quickly forget about it as they continue to follow the story. I've added nothing "dream-like" to Ibsen's text.) Was *Master Builder Solness* ever intended to be credible as a realistic drama, a story that takes place in the real world? I wonder. In the real world, do certain architects decide that instead of building houses, they want to build palaces that stand firmly in the middle of the sky? There *is* a story, of course there is, but the shape of the play is not the shape of the story, it's the shape of a dream, a dream in which apparently every element in Halvard Solness's life is included and examined, a dream in which moral and quasi-philosophical questions take on a palpable, almost bodily life of their own and wrestle with all the many human beings who move through the dream. And, as is natural in a dream, all of these moral and quasi-philosophical questions are layered on top of one another faster than they can be answered or even fully explored, while at the same time the developments in Solness's life, the "story" of the crazily proliferating events unfolding in the various rooms of his tormented house, are flying inexorably forward at a terrifying speed, somehow entirely out of rhythm with all the feverish speculations that are rushing through his mind about his journey in the world and his own impending death.

In other words, *Master Builder Solness* is not a clever theatrical machine whose central purpose is to ensnare and entertain an audience for a couple of hours. It is clearly a reverie in which an anguished author worries aloud to himself, through the medium of a play, about everything in the world that he finds most baffling and confounding. He isn't kidding! And so the play isn't constructed the way plays are normally constructed. It doesn't mold itself to the form of the events it describes but bulges out to encompass abstract thoughts that are thrown into the air by the things that happen. It doesn't seek in the usual way to compel our curiosity and attention by involving us in a plot that develops logically step by step. It doesn't seek in the usual way to enlist our sympathy for the central character, so that we identify with his struggles and yearn for a good outcome for him in all his endeavors. By the time Ibsen wrote this particular play, he was beyond all that.

In other words, as a drama, *Master Builder Solness* is terribly odd and hard to explain. As a dream, it actually makes perfect sense.

This is particularly true when we consider the subject of Hilde Wangel—the heart of the play. And of course one can interpret Hilde as a real person—for example, as an obsessed pre-teenager who seduces an older man, follows him, and murders him, or, alternatively, as the victim of an incident of sexual abuse who finally takes revenge on the man who abused her. But these interpretations of the character of Hilde would not lead an audience into the particular forest of subjects into which Ibsen wanted us to walk and wander. *Master Builder Solness* is not really a story about a man who committed one fateful act, kissing an underaged girl, or a story about a man who had a fateful experience, meeting a strange girl who was determined to kiss *him*. Hide certainly behaves in many ways like a real person, and the play certainly tells the very involving story of a love triangle, in which a man falls in love with a stranger and considers the possibility of running away with her and leaving his wife—but at the same time Hilde functions in the play as a supernatural figure and as a manifestation of Halvard Solness's mind. And while some people have seen Hilde as a dark spirit—a malevolent creature who first tried to kill Solness when she was twelve years old (before she had ever even met him, actually) and who finally comes to his own home to finish the job—André always saw Hilde much more as a spirit of light, a good angel, a benevolent figure whose main reason for coming to earth was simply to help Halvard Solness to die—perhaps even to help him to die with some of the issues in his life resolved. And certainly, whether he resolves any of the issues in his life or not, he most definitely faces them and ponders them inside of his dream, and he struggles to see if he *can* resolve them. The play itself faces these issues and ponders them—but it *doesn't* resolve them. And Solness's death is in a way an expression of the fact that, in the time available in the dream, the time available in Solness's life, the time available in the play, they could *not* be resolved. Solness, having climbed the tower, could not possibly come down, leave his wife, and take Hilde as a lover, nor could he reject Hilde and stay with his wife, and so falling off the tower, death, was the only option possible for him. Nor could Ibsen resolve all the moral and philosophical questions raised by the play, which is one reason why the play is so very disturbing and has never been Ibsen's most popular play.

Strangely, seeing *Master Builder Solness* as a dream also helps us to recognize the elements in this nineteenth-century play that have a striking significance for our own time.

In the world I personally live in—let's say, the apparently sophisticated circles of New York City in 2014—the story of Hilde leading Solness to his death might seem melodramatic. The story of an older man infatuated with a girl of twenty-two might seem predictable. Neither a fear of heights nor a tendency to get dizzy would expose a person in my world to mockery or contempt, and no one I know would find the issue of whether a person was able to climb up a tower to be an important measure of someone's character.

But in the world of our deepest thoughts, in the world of our dreams, the symbols, the images, and the obsessions of Ibsen's play are potent and real. No matter what we're thinking about during the day, when we fall asleep at night, we may very well find ourselves climbing up a tower, and it may very well be an absolutely terrifying experience. *Master Builder Solness* is a dream about the possibility of spiritual transformation. And Halvard Solness, the vain, destructive, dangerous male, desperate because power seems to be slipping from his grasp—the out-of-control giant whose quest for dominance threatens the existence of everything and everyone around him—is quintessentially the figure who today, in our world, needs to be spiritually transformed.

In *Master Builder Solness*, Ibsen and Solness plunge with both feet into the male fantasy of being saved and redeemed by the love of a young girl. Indeed, the story that's told is, more precisely, the fantasy in which an older man is saved not just by a young girl, but by a young girl who falls in love with him after a sexual episode between them—an episode that has occurred when he was an adult and she was a child. And when Hilde and Solness discuss "the Vikings," the episode is indirectly alluded to by both characters as a "violation."

And yet few writers of either sex have gone farther than Henrik Ibsen (author of *A Doll's House*) in escaping from fantasies and painting a harshly truthful portrait of the monstrous male and the Male Principle (the principle of the conqueror, the despoiler, the maker of war, the destroyer of Nature, a Principle that in practice can generously enlist both sexes), and never more so than in *Master Builder Solness*.

Of course the dream is about death, but the imminence of death leads the dream in a direction we couldn't have predicted. Halvard Solness resents younger people. Their health and strength are a reminder that his own health and strength are gradually declining, and that unlike those lucky younger people, who can spend their days in carefree enjoyment of the pleasures of life, he will very soon be pitilessly forced off the edge of the planet, down into death. But in his panic, he has a very surprising reaction, because he cries out in his dream not only to be rescued from unhappiness but also to be changed. He cries out for one last chance to escape from the cage of his own nastiness, the cage of the grasping and heartless self.

The play could be seen as perhaps illogical and self-contradictory. It seems to mock Aline for her belief that "obligation," our duty to others, ought to be the unquestioned bedrock of all of our lives. It begs us to consider the possibility that rather than cleaving to obligation and misery, we ought to reach for ecstasy. And yet one can't watch the play without feeling that Aline is the one truly admirable person whom we see portrayed, that is to say, apart from Dr. Herdal, whom we come to know much less well, but who also seems more guided by obligation than by any Nietzschean drive toward joy. The play questions the value of domestic life and suggests that we ought to seek "the impossible," and that the only structures that can truly contain human happiness are "palaces that stand firmly in the middle of the sky"—yet it refuses to define those palaces or that "impossible," and Solness's search for the transcendent leads only to death. But a dream exists so that it can think about things. It doesn't need to reach conclusions, and when it contradicts itself, it's doing exactly what it has to do, because this is precisely how thinking proceeds.

I decided to change the title of the play a bit, finally, because I couldn't defend the claim that what I'd done was a pure translation. André suggested the title *A Master Builder*.

And then Jonathan Demme watched some of our work on André's production-that-was-never-produced, and he said, "Let's film this." A few extra twists turned the text you're now holding into a screenplay, and the madly burning inspiration of that joyful mad scientist of film, Jonathan Demme, turned André's creation into a movie.

What you have in your hands now is the text of a play, suitable for being performed by anyone who has the nerve to try it. My probably "impossible" hope—my palace standing firmly in the middle of the sky—is that Ibsen will eventually accept this text as his own work and that he'll ultimately tell me that he's pleased by it.

April 2014
New York City